A
MATTER
OF
CHOICE

A
MATTER
OF
CHOICE

THE EFFECTS OF

DAILY CHOICES

CHRISTIANS MAKE

THOMAS
NICHOLS

Pleasant Word
A Division of WinePress Group
PW

ISBN 13: 978-1-4141-1523-8
ISBN 10: 1-4141-1523-7
Library of Congress Catalog Card Number: 2009906693

CONTENTS

INTRODUCTION

We cannot live for ourselves alone. Our lives are connected by a thousand invisible threads, and along those sympathetic fibers, our actions run as causes and return to us as results.

—Herman Melville

I F WE COULD really understand the concept of how our lives are connected by thousands of invisible threads, then we would begin to understand that the minute things we do have enormous consequences both in our small world and in the larger one. We might not think that as our everyday lives are mostly routine.

What possible good or harm can come from the minute actions we do everyday? So I threw a piece of paper out the car window, so I ran a red light, so I didn't pick up the clothes I accidentally knocked off the clothes rack, so I didn't give to the Salvation Army or the church or the United Fund, so what if I exceeded my credit limit, I will pay it back, so what if I take my entitled sick days? And the list could string out into a thousand other things that we think are insignificant actions but return to us in the higher cost of maintaining a societal infrastructure. There is power in numbers—power in multiplication. And that power and those numbers have positive and negative effects.

Conversely, we can do good things. As John Wesley put it, "doing all the good we can all the time we can, for as ever as long as we can" has its own power in numbers. Unfortunately, the bad things in life get the press, the good don't. "The evil that men do live after them, the good is interred with their bones," Shakespeare noted. The good we are instructed to do and not the evil, but as a matter of choice, we can choose to do either.

Coming to the knowledge that choices, however small or large, have power and that power runs as causes and returns to us as results, we might think that somehow, someone or something is allowing those choices to occur. It is more than the fact that we are endowed with certain inalienable rights; we are endowed by God to have liberty of choice.

The power of one's choice is significant if not the most empowering realization we will ever have. What is striking about our free will, or the power to affect the affairs of our life, is the tremendous responsibility attached to that gift and the humbling effect it should place on us. If we wanted a wish granted at the start of our life, and had the wisdom to ask, it would probably include free will or the freedom to make our own choices. And, indeed that is what God has granted us. The idea of the power of choice and one's freedom to choose is one of God's greatest gifts to mankind. Not only did God grant freedom of choice to His created image—man, but He granted freedom of choice to the heavenly beings as well. Lucifer, the son of morning as Isaiah stated, was the first to commit the sin of pride and rebellion against God when he said "…I will ascend into heaven I will exalt my throne above the stars of God; I will sit also upon the mount of the congregation, in the sides of he north, I will ascend above the heights of the clouds, I will be like the Most High" (Isaiah 14:12-14 KJV).

Therefore if God let all creation have freewill, then that gift is bestowed upon all of us. If freedom of choice is sacred to Him and He will not interfere with it, then it should be sacred to us and instill in us the gravity of proper choices.

What a sobering thought! Most of us go though life making choices, some serious, but most not. Generally, we make innocent and simple choices for others and ourselves such as what to have for lunch or where to stop for gas or what television program to watch or what shall we wear. Other more serious choices and decisions are a bit more sobering: what college to go to, shall I get this job or that, join the military, pursue a career, or get married. Sometimes there comes a decision that is life altering, emotionally disturbing, or even life-threatening to others and us. These will form our future, our life, and our destiny. In this writing, we are concerned with important choices. The simple ones take care of themselves. Most all choices are ours and ours alone to make, and generally only we can make them. No one else can make them for us. The resulting outcome can be profound.

As a personal example, sometime ago I had a hard career decision to make. I had been offered the possibility of creating a major exhibition for a newly-built museum in a Midwestern city. I had lived and worked in Pittsburgh and had a good job and was content with my life. The new job possibility would require me to quit that good job and start my own business. I had the experience and the knowledge to create this exhibit, but so many issues were confounding: did I really want to leave my secure job with my relatively good salary and venture out in the unknown? And second, did I really want to embark on a project that would overwhelm and be a life-altering venture for the rest of my work life?

My wife and I pondered, prayed, sorted out the issues, and finally, after many agonizing hours, days, and weeks, decided to do it.

To make a long story short, I quit my good job, I designed and built and installed the exhibit over a period of five years, and it was a rave success.

In retrospect, I never looked back. I never regretted my choice. I never regretted the hard work, the stressful hours of uncertainty and fear of time crunch, the expenses, the logistical issues, the living for a period in another city. It was a life-altering change, but a rewarding one with unprecedented experiences and travel.

There was power in my choice. There are similar examples shared by each of us. We all have our stories to tell of the simple, the complex, of life-changing choices.

There is power in our choices—profoundly so. Certainly there is power in good, positive, deliberate choice, and there is also power in not choosing. In some situations, not choosing *is* choosing. Take voting for instance. We can choose to vote or not; both are choosing. But choosing not to vote is the worst kind of choice. When we choose not to vote we do not exercise our democratic right and opportunity, nor do we choose the right people for the job. We might say, "it doesn't matter anyway, they all are unsuitable," or "there are no good choices." That may be true, but active, interested people can change outcomes. There are many nations whose governments don't permit voting or the ability to voice an opinion, or even the basic exercise of human rights. Would we prefer that? And if we don't agree that "not choosing is choosing," then we are indifferent, and that's a choice.

Reflecting on the events of the Garden of Eden as recorded in Genesis chapter three, we see the power of choice exercised to the fullest extent. God commanded Adam "you are free to eat from any tree in the garden; but you must not eat from the tree of the knowledge of good and evil, for when you eat of it you will surely die." Later, Eve was encouraged to eat of the forbidden fruit by the serpent who said, "you will not surely die, for God knows that when you eat of it your eyes will be opened and you will be like gods, knowing good and evil."

What a decisive moment in time! That one momentous choice has afflicted humankind ever since. It is history's most consequential choice. "When the woman saw that the fruit of the tree was good for food and pleasing to the eye, and also desirable for wisdom, she took some and ate it." Had Eve known the gravity of that one choice and the consequences of that single act, would she have done it? We don't know, but we can suspect that she made a choice for the moment without regard to consequence. We all do that. We want instant gratification even if we know the consequences or suspect that we might get away with it. I'm not stereotyping all humankind for we are not all alike, but history does prove the overwhelming impulse to ignore consequences.

Eve was warned by God Himself not to eat. She ignored God. The fruit satisfied all human desires—food, visual stimulation, and wisdom. The serpent said, "You will be like gods, knowing the difference between good and evil."

We see the interplay between the voice of warning (God) and the voice of desire (Satan). One says do and the other says don't, and the attractiveness of the wrong won out. Eve heard the voices of good and evil and was influenced by both. In the end, she made her own decision to do the wrong thing—rebel against God. And the sin that affected her afflicts all mankind.

INTRODUCTION

We all know. We are all contaminated with sin. All the generations since Adam and Eve know that now. We struggle to do good but evil comes easy. We have to teach goodness but wrong is the whole of us. It is the curse of rebellion.

Who is in control of our choices? Are we? Are there forces in and outside of us? Both voices of good and evil persuaded Eve, but was it she and she alone who made the ultimate choice?

We have to acknowledge that we are drawn by a number of influences (forces) inside and outside of ourselves: traditions, society, culture, peers, family, religion, associations, superstitions, astrology, our own conscience, the spirit of God, and the "evil" one. Where is our own identity among all these helps or hindrances? After all, we desire, have wants, needs, ambitions, and want to be our own person. Ultimately though, we have responsibility for all our internal and external motivations. That is as it should be. We, therefore, can choose to let any of these help or hinder us.

Influences outside of us are good and bad. We want family and the benefits the family unit brings to society. We want help; life is too difficult to do it alone. We want teachers, mentors, advisors, friends, and spiritual guidance. We always need those, not only in our formative years, but also throughout all of life. We use these as supporters, not our decision makers. We are still autonomous and fully responsible for whatever choices we make.

Originally, this writing was never intended to be a religious work or a spiritual guide. It was merely to ponder the significance of choice and the wonderful opportunity that power affords us, but as the writing progressed, it became clear the work had to be from a Christian perspective. There is no other way to address a blessing such as free choice, the power to choose or our personal freedoms, without the input of divine wisdom. After all, it is God's gift to us and it is His institution.

In our wonderment of why God doesn't intervene in such and such circumstance or the evils of the world or poverty or any other situation seemingly out of our control, we have to remember that God has granted us the best gift in life, the ability to choose. That blessing is not on specific individuals, but for all of mankind. All the evil or good that exists in the world was a direct result of someone's choice. All the evil or good that continues in the world is a collective result of our present choices. Soberly, that implies and applies the burden of responsibility squarely on our shoulders.

As a human race, we could choose to eradicate poverty, educate the masses, live peacefully among ourselves, and solve the complex issues of society. History says we didn't and biblical prophecy says we won't. However, we could if we so chose.

John Ormsbee Simonds says in his book *Landscape Architecture:*

> Down through the dim chaotic ages, the force of the human mind has met and mastered situation after situation and has raised us (through his planning process) to a position of supremacy over all the creatures of the earth.
>
> We have in fact inherited the earth. This vast globe on which we dwell is ours, ours to develop further, as an agreeable living environment. Surely, we with our twinkling minds should by now have created for ourselves a paradise on this earth. (pg. 4)

Does that dishearten us? Does it incite action? Impel us to do good? Does it motivate us to conquer the forces that prevent positive good on the earth? Does it instill desire to address global warming? Addictive drugs? Aids? Eradicate cancer? Oppression? Does it cause us to wonder where we have gone wrong? After all, the world is ours to manage, conquer, subdue, and exercise stewardship. God handed the world to us—He made everything just for us.

Choices: The Categories

This writing is not a definitive answer on the matter of choosing, but rather designed to help us think about the incredible gift given to us that permit the freedom to choose. Hopefully we will reflect on the implications of our choices and be conscious of the gravity and seriousness of that power.

We each have our own methods of choosing and arriving at decisions. Those elements of process—choices or the lack thereof—fall into many categories. The extent of these filter into areas not typically associated with decision-making but certainly attach them logically. These chapters ponder the variety of choices that confront us.

Every day we make choices that lead toward decisions, some with purpose, some not. Some are made for us either with or without our knowledge, consent, or our cooperation. Some we shun or express with indifference. Some are quick and decisive. Some are seemingly made without thought (without purpose)—spontaneous if you will. Some we agonize over, lose sleep over, worry over. Some decisions take years to come to a decisive moment in time (delayed choice), some have life and death consequences, some have moral and ethical implications and some we just don't know why we chose what we chose.

The use of language between choices and decisions are close relatives. While choices and decisions are not synonymous, both words are used here to describe the mental process of choosing. To make a decision requires many choices, options, and facts. Those are the ingredients for making rational and correct decisions. Knowledge is foremost. Often time, choices and decisions are not that deliberate. Some are impulsive, irrational, without thought, and plain wrong. Yet some decisions of critical matters are very methodical, thoughtful, incorporate a host of experts or advisors and have all the facts and knowledge to bear. This is the correct process toward right decision making. Even when we think correct decisions and choices have been made, history will prove the rightness or wrongness of our actions.

Generally we choose for ourselves the good things, or perceived good, based upon "incentives" as described in the book *Freakonomics* by Steven D. Levitt and Stephen J. Dubner. In it, the authors say people are motivated by incentives. That is true, whether they are good or bad, incentives push us toward both wise and unwise choices. We want results that make us feel good: food, satisfaction, a clear conscience, a physical or psychological desire or need, security, comfort, or even a drug fix.

Following the logical process, once the choices are evaluated and the decision made, there is the end result or consequence of the choice. Does my decision end with the choice? Is it the beginning? Does it require some commitment on my part, a consequence? Often times the follow-up, implementation, or aftermath of a decision is the most difficult and consequential part of the whole decision process. It may require a sacrifice, a commitment, a long-term relationship, a promise, a contract, or a possibility of putting one's life on the line.

Remember, the invisible threads that weave us together run as causes also return to us as results. There is nothing we do that won't affect others, or conversely, everything we do affects others.

CHOICES WITH PURPOSE

No individual has any right to come into the world and go out of it without leaving behind him distinct and legitimate reasons for having passed through it.

—George Washington Carver

IT STARTS WITH a spark, an interest, a goal, a commitment toward a desired end. We may not see the end and maybe only the beginning of a dream, but it drives, motivates, and captures our spirit. The spark is different for all of us. It may ignite from parents, from our own interests, from teachers, from destiny, or from Providence, but the vision of that freedom, that symphony, that search, that invention, that moon, that mountain, that education, that book, drives us toward purpose.

Most of our choices do have positive purposes. When we have a goal in mind, a specific plan to go from point A to point B, there is purpose, focus, and mission in life. We all need that. The commitment to constant self-improvement is essential to give perspective to one's life. It is a force that cannot be reckoned with, a force that changes things.

Let us address the opposite for a moment—life without purpose. Yes we can choose not to seek the best for ourselves: to squander our lives away, to be content with life as it is. We can choose to go through life without a dream, a mission, or real purpose, and we might be content with that for a while until such time we realize life is passing us by. I've known a few who seemingly have none of those goals or mission instincts.

They have no desire to be competitive, succeed, excel in school, or do anything other than just exist. The irony of this scenario is that these individuals are often content. They are not driven by the need to know more or the need to know the news or weather, but are satisfied to simply eat, be healthy, bask in the affection of family, and accept life as it is. In many respects that lifestyle is not without worthy consideration.

Rick Warren, author of *The Purpose Driven Life*, would say that, "without purpose, life is motion without meaning, activity without direction, and events without reason. Without a purpose, life is trivial, petty and pointless." Beyond the truth of Rick Warren's statement is the fact that people without purpose, especially kids, are more likely to get into trouble, experiment with drugs, alcohol, smoking, sex, and crime than those who have a genuine goal in life. It harkens back to the old statement of "an idle mind is…."

What things strip our desire, deaden our motivation, or kill our spirit on the road to purpose? Society and our culture do have a numbing effect on us, especially for our youth. Life is so fast-paced with school, jobs, commuting, games, TV, sports, extra-curricular activities, and entertainment, to the point they (we) are never satisfied with idleness and always looking to the next "fun" thing. The lack of activity quickly produces boredom and worse, stifles our creativity. Busyness addresses the immediate and distorts the vision and purpose of our lives and then quickly develops into habit. Once habit occurs our choices become demands of the moment and repetition.

Yet in all this, we can rise above the negativity, the indifference of society and the humdrum of life. Not all of us will be the greats of the world. Most of us are common folk, but we can be what we want to be, what we choose to be, what God wants us to be.

We can learn much from history's greats: Beethoven, Salk, Patrick Henry, Abraham Lincoln, Churchill, the Wright Brothers, Washington, Helen Keller, Christopher Reeve, and many others. Gilbert Highet says in his book, *Man's Unconquerable Mind,* "we can never tell how great thinkers emerge…They do not grow like trees; they cannot be bred like selected animals. People are not born thoughtless or thoughtful. They become thoughtless or thoughtful." Similarly, people are not born with purpose or without, they become purposeful or purposeless.

If we look at the many lives that have contributed to the betterment of humanity, the discoverers, inventors and explorers, art and literary contributors, we would have to be in awe over their tenacity and persistence of work to sort out the problems of their inventions and ideas. The solutions of their dreams and our own dreams are reachable by our willingness and choice to work toward those goals.

Life with purpose can come from the most meager of beginnings. The story of George Washington Carver is a prime example. He was born in 1864 in obscurity, poverty, and slavery. Yet he grew up an ambitious black youngster in white country and found the wherewithal to get an education. He persisted in getting a high school education and then later, amid hardships and prejudicial putdowns, a college degree. Because he was sickly as a youth, he became skilled in plants and agricultural research rather than the physical demands of farm life. Much later in his life he developed 300 uses of the peanut and joined the facility at Tuskegee Institute, a black research institution.

Just as George Washington Carver legitimized his place in the world, we individuals who are slow to find purpose might well gain insight into greater possibilities by the story of Carver.

Take Thomas Edison, as another example. The story of his invention of the incandescent lamp is remarkable. It is not only remarkable in the sense of his tireless trail and error methods, but his work ethic as well. Ron Clark, in his book titled *Edison,* remarked, "He worked on relentlessly, experimenting with material after material, producing filaments of different thicknesses and in different shapes. Some were too fragile to be satisfactorily sealed into the glass bulbs. Others burned out almost as soon as the current was passed through them… He kept doggedly on." (*Edison,* Ron W. Clark, pg. 96, G.F. Putnum's Son, New York.)

Aided with a new Sprengel air pump, which enabled him to produce an almost perfect vacuum, he soon found that hermetically sealed bulbs would retain this high vacuum for long periods if not indefinitely. He always felt that carbon was ideal for a filament, provided a proper vacuum could be obtained.

Edison could have given up. He chose not to. This was a discovery by persistence, tenacity, a driven spirit, and an ultimate goal in mind.

To Edison, there was an answer to be found and he would not give up until the desired end. He made a choice.

There are other individuals who had similar purpose: the Wright Brothers, Fleming, Columbus, Salk, Carver, and a host of others. We might ask, what are the ingredients that come together to solve problems that arrive at solutions? Of course, there's knowledge, but other factors come into play also, and most have to do with our own personalities: persistence, patience, tenacity, a tireless work ethic, and sacrifice. Often it is trial and error, serendipity, coincidence, luck, chance, and divine providence. But without sufficient knowledge of the subject at hand, the accidents of discovery might continue to go undiscovered.

In the Christian arena, choosing not to have purpose is to be ineffective, a non-productive Christian and a poor worker in God's kingdom. "Where there is no vision, the people perish; but he that keepeth the law, happy is he." (Proverbs 29:18 KJV). Further, and more serious for us, is that we do not allow God to do His work in our lives. In *The Purpose-Driven Life*, Warren describes how to find our purpose in His purpose, so that together our will is submitted to His will. That unity is a life altering union of Master and servant.

With the many choices that confront us, choice with a purpose is the ultimate and desired kind. We each have a talent. Some know it immediately, some take years to discover it, but coming to the realization that we have the freedom, opportunity, and responsibility to make our own choices and discover our own destiny, is, profoundly our personal choice. There is the ultimate power in that kind of choice. It is power without hindrance.

Whether in life, in the church, or in our Christian walk, people with purpose make individuals virtually unstoppable.

CHAPTER 2

CHOICES MADE FOR US BY PEOPLE AND CIRCUMSTANCES

This is as true in everyday life as it is in battle: we are given one life and the decision is ours whether to wait for circumstances to make up our mind, or whether to act, and in acting, to live.

—Omar N. Bradley

W E ARE WHO we are for many reasons. The influence of family and the values they bring to the individual is an encompassing and enduring force. We don't get to choose who we are: what our background is, our color, creed, or religion. We inherit these.

Our religious, political, and social values are a result of being raised in a certain geographic location, ethnic background, and family values. If we think we have chosen who we are, that is probably not a realistic view of ourselves. We may choose who we continue to be, but not what or who we are. Knowing this has tremendous personal realization. We are less likely to be critical and judgmental of others if we recognize who and why we are who we are.

Historically we, as United States citizens, could at this moment speak another language, have another religion, be of any color, be part of another political system or social system if we had been explored, invaded, and colonized by any other political system other than the British. If world events had gone other directions we might speak Spanish, French, Dutch, or Portuguese at this moment in time. Individually, even if we had been raised differently, in another geographic location, under another religion, we would not be the person we are.

We might then ask the question, is who I am a result of luck, randomness, being in the right place at the right time, or conversely, the wrong place at the wrong time, or are our lives prearranged by providence? It is something to ponder.

In a sense it doesn't matter who we are, how we got here or why. Our lives are now ours to manage, to develop, to enrich. Under this unique government we can choose to be whatever we want.

Oftentimes in our everyday living, circumstances, or life if you will, can waylay our purposes faster than any other known stumbling block. What did John Lennon say? "Life happens while you are making other plans."

There are many choices made for us that are not our doing—some we willfully go along with and some not. Children depend on the choices, decisions, and demands of parents and caregivers for their well-being until such time as they are autonomous. Students attend schools where knowledgeable teachers guide and direct the educational elements in their lives. Young people may not want to be in school as they typically would rather be elsewhere, but it is a necessary confine. Governments are instituted among people to provide the free exercise of life, liberty, and the pursuit of happiness. Corporations and employers give jobs and provide our economic stability. The country and individuals depend on them for the economy and financial security. Society and laws dictate our conduct, which we often rebel against, but participate in for our general well-being: we go along grudgingly or happily for the betterment of our quality of life.

Tradition and parental influence have a stronger hold on us than we realize or care to admit and can have a lasting influence. Tradition often predetermines our own choices and dominates the simplest of decisions. Tradition can be a drug that chains us to medieval thought and strips us of our freedom.

However, family, ethnicity, religion, and traditions taken in a positive and productive light can and do have great value and add to the quality of life. Cultural, ethnic, and family traditions are a treasure and something sure to be proud of. The key to our choices and how they relate to tradition is the wisdom to hold on to the good, and frees you of the holds on your life. The phrase, "we have always done it that way," may be something to keep as a tradition or it could be an imprisoning device.

Choices made for us under these scenarios are the good kind. Good in the sense that we are secure, have freedom, have opportunities, and have choices. In truth we would not prefer it otherwise.

Choices made for us are a necessary mechanism for civil and social stability even though Americans in general are independent-minded individuals. We are free spirited, innovative, and ingenious. We have the attitude that free choice and liberty are our inalienable rights and American mentality: that is instilled in our very existence.

The so-called American Dream comes from the mentality that "there is no limit to what anyone can have or achieve." With education, hard work, and a little bit of luck, we can fulfill that dream of home ownership, two cars in the garage, TVs, and all the spice of life. That may be our modern day conception of it, but the real idea of the American Dream as coined by James Truslow Adams in his book *The Epic of America* is expressed as:

> …there has been also the American dream, that dream of a land in which life should be better and richer and fuller for every man, with opportunity for each according to his ability or achievement.…it is not a dream of motorcars and high wages merely, but a dream of a social order in which each man and each woman shall be able to attain to the fullest stature of which they are innately capable, and be recognized by others for what they are, regardless of the fortuitous circumstances of birth or position. (pg. 317)

The social order Adams spoke about was wrought by our founding fathers. They had a vision of a land that should be better and richer and fuller for every man who works for it. That vision is summed in the Preamble in our very own Constitution:

> We the people of the United States, in Order to form a more perfect Union, establish Justice, insure domestic Tranquility, provide for the common defense, promote the general Welfare, and secure the

Blessings of Liberty to ourselves and our Posterity, do ordain and establish this Constitution for the United States of America.

The American Dream as written by Adams is possible because we have a government that fosters that dream. We, as Americans, do indeed have a unique government. It has been fashioned from a relative handful of individuals who sought freedom above all else and bought it with blood, sweat, and tears.

The image of the American Dream plus hard times and famine in Europe are what drove immigrants to seek the fulfillment of those instant riches. They arrived by the millions at Ellis Island searching for a better life. The supposed land of opportunity was there, but it was laden with hard work, prejudice, poverty, and immense struggle. Some made it—most didn't.

Immigration policies and requirements have changed since the influx of Europeans sought labor in the Americas around the turn of the twentieth century. While the American Dream is still coveted by some, the United States is not high on the list of desired countries in which to live. We Americans still see our country as the land of opportunity, but not all can or will take advantage of it. Also, not all peoples of the world, all six billion of us, have opportunities or choices available to us—some are fortunate, some are not. Many are hampered by the circumstances of political systems of the countries they live in, by poverty, by lack of opportunity, by oppression, or their own inability or desire to manage their own choices.

Often, circumstance confines us and takes away our freedom: slavery, prison, poverty, ignorance, cults, chemical dependency, or other physiological, psychological, or sociological hindrances rob a person of making free choices about their lives. Could we safely say that we who lack the ability to make choices for ourselves are victims of circumstance, or is it our own creation, our own choice? Isn't there always choice?

While there are many non-freedoms that strip man of his needs, "poverty is man's most powerful and massive affliction," says John Kenneth Galbraith. Poverty is the most pervasive and enduring oppression presently occurring. While there are many causes of poverty, it is an ageless phenomenon and a byproduct of oppression, famine, unemployment, climate, geographical location, and the inability of governments to enable people to secure the necessities of life. Oppressive governments and those who devalue the sanctity of human rights and strip a society of opportunity offer little hope to people under their rule. These certainly offer few choices to individuals. It is a prison of sorts, the worst kind. The individual has no recourse to alter his plight. Generally, governments govern for the good of the people. They should make or must make decisions for people who can't make decisions or choices for themselves. This is as it should be, but often is not reality. We know of governments of the past and the present that do otherwise.

Barbara Tuchman, in her book *The March of Folly* says,

> The overall responsibility of power is to govern as reasonably as possible in the interest of the state and its citizens. A duty in that process is to keep well-informed, to heed information, to keep mind and judgment open and to resist the insidious spell of wooden-headedness. If the mind is open enough to perceive that a given policy is harming rather than serving self-interest, and self-confident enough to acknowledge it, and wise enough to reverse it, that is the summit in the art of government. (pg.32)

Today, approximately one-half the world's population is impoverished. That is 2.8 billion out of the six billion living on the earth. That is almost one out of every two individuals who subsist on virtually nothing. What an astounding number. What recourse do the poor have in those situations? Not much, I'm afraid.

In the Old Testament, the Bible says, "There will always be poor people in the land. Therefore I command you to be openhanded toward your bothers and toward the poor and needy in your land" (Deuteronomy 15:11). And Jesus said, "The poor you have with you always."

Historically, the "haves" always dominate the "have nots." It is a reality. However, those of us who have been given much have the greater responsibility to feed, relieve, and support those less fortunate. It is our Christian and humanitarian obligation.

Reaction to Circumstances

Two men look out through the same bars: one sees mud, and the other stars.

—Robert Louis Stevenson

Stevenson's quote says that we each see our plights, misfortunes, and oppressions differently. One will give up and resign to confinement and the other will see possibilities. There are evidences of individuals who found opportunity amidst the harshest of conditions. *Pilgrim's Progress* was written while John Bunyan was in confinement for almost twelve years. The apostle Paul wrote the bulk of the New Testament, while enduring shipwrecks, prison, beatings and persecution; the apostle John wrote *Revelation* while exiled to the Island of Patmos; Anne Frank wrote one the most powerful diaries ever written while hiding from the Nazis; Dietrich Bonhoeffer, a theologian, was an outspoken critic of the Jewish persecution in Nazi Germany and was confined, persecuted, and hanged before the liberation of the Jews in 1945.

There were many others who saw and chose opportunity while being oppressed or imprisoned.

As individuals and free agents in this God-given liberty, where is our free will amid the demands of society, of oppressors, of things out of our control? As children and adults we get into situations where few choices are a reality. What if a person or group of persons is in a position of having limited choices?

I have taken four stories: one story comes from my own experience, the second is from the scriptural story of Joseph, the third is from Dr. Frankl's book, *Man's Search for Meaning,* and the fourth is an excerpt from the book *Ghost Soldiers.*

Out of my personal history there is a story about Sam. Sam was our helper on my dad's small southern farm. He was not indentured by any stretch of the term; it was an agreement between two individuals: one needing labor, the other needing food and shelter. Sam lived in a two-room shack on our property and he and his wife did farm duties while my father worked in the local textile mill. The farm dabbled in cotton, sweet potatoes, peanuts, beans, corn, turnips, and others.

Sam had nothing, but he seemed content from my youthful eye. His food and his living quarters were provided, but beyond that I don't believe he had much money. He certainly did not have a car, and depended upon my Dad to take him places or he walked.

When I look back at this scenario, I wonder why Sam was content with that lifestyle. Perhaps he wasn't. Perhaps he had no choice. Perhaps he didn't even think of other possibilities for himself or family. He was uneducated, poor, had no opportunities for betterment, no transportation, no marketable skills other than farm work.

Did Sam have choices? Could he have bettered himself? Could he have acquired an education which might have enabled him to get a better job, a better life? Did he have the motivation or the recognition of a better life? Would any of us have acted differently given similar circumstances? Can we say he had few choices? He did, but they were severely limited. He had a choice to be content or not, to be ambitious or not, to acquire education or not, to seek help or not. If he had the opportunity to state his case, he might not agree with me. After all, it was the south, in the 1940s, and the white/black social relationships were less than equal.

Consider the biblical story of Joseph. This account is from the 37th Chapter of Genesis. "Joseph, a young man of seventeen, was tending the flocks with his brothers, the sons of Bilhah and the sons of Zilpah, his father's wives, and brought their father a bad report about them. Now Jacob loved Joseph more than any of his other sons, because he had been born to him in his old age; and he made a richly ornamental robe for him." (The fabled coat of many colors). "When his brothers saw that their father loved him more than any of them, they hated him and could not speak a kind word to him." Later, Joseph had a dream revealing a future prophecy that his brothers would bow down to him.

Envy and jealously burned within the older brothers and they connived to kill Joseph. But the older one, Ruben, convinced the others to leave him in a pit and abandon him. Meanwhile, a caravan of Midianites came by and the brothers sold Joseph into slavery and he was taken to Egypt. An Egyptian official, Potiphar, had bought Joseph from his Midianite captors and took him into his household. Potiphar saw how Joseph was favored by God and prospered in everything he did. Potiphar made him overseer of the entire household. Joseph was an upright and God-fearing man who did right in every situation.

Joseph was a handsome man and physically attractive to Potiphar's wife. She tried repeatedly to seduce him, but he resisted her advances. She became angry and falsely accused him of rape. When the master heard his wife's tale of the supposed rape, Potiphar was enraged and had Joseph thrown into prison among the other king's prisoners. Still, the Lord was with him, and a prison guard showed him favor—and put him in charge of the entire prison. Yet, Joseph was in confinement a very long time—years in fact.

As time passed, the king's cupbearer and baker offended Pharaoh and they were put into custody under the assignment of Joseph. As the two were in prison, they each had dreams but no interpretation. Joseph, learning of their anxiousness of their dreams said that only God could reveal the secret of their visions. Joseph then, with God's revelation, told the meaning of the dreams to the cupbearer and the baker. The interpretation was that the cupbearer's life would be saved but the baker would hang.

On the king's birthday, the cupbearer and the baker were held up in front of the king's officials. The King restored the cupbearer but the baker was hanged, which was Joseph's interpretation of their dreams.

Joseph had asked the cupbearer to mention him to the king to offer favor on Joseph's behalf, however, the cupbearer forgot. This slight of mind cost Joseph another two years in prison. Meanwhile, Pharaoh himself had dreams no one could interpret. When the cupbearer learned of Pharaoh's plight, he remembered Joseph and told Pharaoh that there was one in prison who could interpret his dreams. Pharaoh summoned Joseph and God enabled him to explain Pharaoh's dream of the impending seven years of famine in Egypt. There would be seven years of plenty and seven years of famine. As a result of that interpretation, Pharaoh made Joseph overseer of the whole land of Egypt.

There are many points to this story and how it relates to choice. Joseph chose to maintain his integrity through the good years and in the difficult ones. The Lord blessed him for it.

This is a biblical account where we see God's involvement in Joseph the man and how that story relates to God's chosen people. We can recount each of our own stories and histories and how God has revealed Himself to us during good and bad times. It is true that if we seek God in everything we do, God will work His plan in and through us. Those are biblical promises.

In life's greatest struggles to maintain one's very existence, account after account testifies that man always has a choice: a choice to hang on to life, or to give up, a choice to give life or to take it. Both of the following examples are about choosing one's destiny.

However free or limited our freedoms are, we are never totally devoid of choices. These stories illustrate the varying circumstances of life including oppression, prisoners of war, poverty, and slavery.

Dr. Viktor Frankl describes in his book *Man's Search for Meaning:*

> We who lived in concentration camps can remember the men who walked through the huts comforting others, giving away their last piece of bread. They may have been few in number, but they offer sufficient proof that everything can be taken from a man but one thing: the last of the human freedoms—to choose one's attitude in any given set of circumstances, to choose one's own way.

> And there were always choices to make. Every day, every hour, offered the opportunity to make a decision, a decision which determined whether you would or would not submit to those powers which threatened to rob you of your very self, your inner freedom; which determined whether or not you would become the plaything of circumstance, renouncing freedom and dignity to become molded into the form of the typical inmate.(pgs. 86-87)

In the book *Ghost Soldiers*, Hampton Sides gives an account of the "Bataan death march" where captured American prisoners were forced to march mile after mile under the most brutish of punishment and then placed in an encampment for years under horrid conditions. Yet many survived under the sheer desire to live; others chose death. The difference between the two, those who chose to live and those who didn't, is a complex psychological process and different for each individual.

Sides describes the following:

> Yet in many cases the act of dying seemed to come by force of will. Every doctor saw it. A patient who was sick but not necessarily terminal would suddenly get an unmistakable look on his face—a million-mile stare, a crushing melancholy, as if to say, "I cannot bear another moment." He would simply give up. Within hours, sometimes within minutes, he'd be dead. The prisoners called it "give-up-itis." The doctors referred to it as "inanition," the absence of spirit. "Living was like holding on to a rope," said one medic. "All you had to do was let go and you were a goner." (pg.109)

In the book *Soul Catcher*, the author's fictional character Rosetta says to Cain, her slave catcher, "Everybody gots a choice…Only person don't is this young'un inside me. He don't have no choice. Can't choose not to come onto this world. Or to come. People got to choose that for him."

Is Rosetta right? Does everyone have a choice?

The Fairness of Life

There have been volumes written about the fairness or unfairness of life. "Why do bad things happen to good people," is explored in a book of the same name written by Harold Kushner; or even, why do good things happen to bad people—these are the unfathomable and unanswerable questions of life. But the godly promises of Scripture are many. "…Never will I leave you; never will I forsake you." (Hebrews 13: 5 NIV) And "yea though I walk through the valley of the shadow of death, I will fear no evil; for thou art with me; thy rod and thy staff they comfort me." (Psalm 23: 4 KJV)

Life is difficult and often unfair. We have both responsibility and comfort in whatever life deals us. Responsibility in that we are charged with certain godly conduct. Comfort in that we have God's promises of assurance and protection that we are His heirs in the family of God. That does not necessarily mean we are favored with good times or an easy life. It may even mean life will be more difficult in our belief system. Joseph did not have an easy life, but he was blessed. Scripture doesn't explain why we may walk through the valley of death, or suffer or starve or be subjected to oppression, but God helps and comforts us during times of struggle.

Obviously there are varied levels of oppression and opportunity depending on circumstances, society, or the country we live in. The poor of Africa is not the same poorness that exists in the United States. They both are classified as poverty but both are different in opportunity. The poor in Africa have less opportunity, less chance, less education, and less future, yet more opportunity for disease, famine, and death. The people have no way of changing their plight. Government, (the same that causes the problem), is the only catalyst for change. At this writing there are eleven-million orphaned children in Africa with no opportunity for a future. Eleven million. They have limited choices.

I've only singled out Africa as an example. It likely is the worst situation in the world, but there are many others who face a world absent of opportunities. By some miracle there could be a change of government, or countries might come to their aid, or some wealthy individual might temporarily offer some relief for a few; but this is a vague reality. It is, however, the responsibility of the privileged to be compassionate, giving, and aiding.

Spiritual Entanglements

For we wrestle not against flesh and blood, but against principalities, against powers, against the rulers of the darkness of this world, against spiritual wickedness in high places.
—Ephesians 6:12 (KJV)

In the spiritual arena, we struggle amid forces of which we may or may not be aware. There are two forces in the world: that of good and of evil. The evil forces are oppressive in the sense that we are held captive by our own wrong choices, by the evil forces, and because we yield to the wrongs that appear right. They manifest themselves in an array of spoilers that waylay our freedoms, our choices, and our opportunities. We need to be clear headed when we suspect our freedom of choice is in jeopardy. Is it by others? If so is it legitimate? Is it oppression? Is it our own choice? Or, is it forces outside of us?

A MATTER OF CHOICE

We are responsible for all the choices of our lives. We may let others make choices for us as we are helpless to do otherwise, or we might manage our choices with all the diligence of a proper steward. When adversities hit us, and they will at some point in our lives, we do indeed have choices in how we deal with whatever mild or hard suffering might occur.

CHAPTER 3

INDIFFERENCE AS A CHOICE

Indifference is the strongest force in the universe. It makes everything it touches meaningless. Love and hate don't stand a chance against it.
— Joan Vinge *The Snow Queen*

Science may have found a cure for most evils; but it has found no remedy for the worst of them all—apathy of human beings.
— Hellen Keller

WHAT IS INDIFFERENCE? Fundamentally we might possess knowledge or be aware of a situation or event or circumstance, but cannot be bothered to apply ourselves to it. Indifference in most situations is a deliberate personal choice of our own. Our lack of involvement occurs for various reasons: we don't have time, don't want to be involved, are not interested, are selfish, or just want to live life without people interfering.

Indifference and its many synonyms—unconcerned, apathetic, incurious, detached, disinterested— are intended to lean toward a definition of purposeful lack of involvement, interest, and concern where participation would normally be expected. We all have a tendency toward indifference to some degree. It is impossible to be involved in every situation. But generally, indifference is a paralyzing phenomenon.

How can we be exposed to repeated forces and opportunities in our life and not be affected by them? We go through life's routines day after day and do it so repeatedly that we become callused or unaffected by them. Does the regimen of day to day routine just glaze us over?. The mask of indifference is subtle, sneaky, unconscious, unrecognizable, and totally absorbing. It breeds coldness, rudeness, selfism, ingratitude, hatred, and disrespect, and spreads ubiquitously into all that we touch or affect.

Society and culture often lead us in the way of indifference. That doesn't excuse us to any degree, but our culture is a breeding ground for indifference. While I would not fault any specific facet of American culture as being the catalyst mind-set of degradation, yet the steady daily diet of exposure to non-stimulating, non-cultural, immoral and non-intellectualism has led us to be materialistic, cold, impersonal, and dull. Indifference blurs the line between right and wrong and breeds those things not right or proper. Indifference numbs us to the point of apathy and therefore in the end, diminishes our choices.

The sheer volume of media messages that come our way every day, whether through magazines, newspapers, radio, or television, anesthetize and desensitize us toward everyday events. The important becomes unimportant.

Not only does media numb us, but the fast-paced lives we live today—the commutes, the routines, the repetition, the survival in the workplace, the pressures, the competition, the lack of proper rest and nutrition—all contribute to our indifference to society.

Take the smoker for instance. Not that I'm singling smoking out as a peeve, but it illustrates the point of indifference.

A smoker is totally out for self-satisfaction. Later, it becomes a habit that turns addictive both physically and mentally. If the habit of smoking would just be a personal thing, without the affect of making others participate in their habit, then it would be that—a personally destructive habit. But smoking is never just personal. It is a communal habit, affecting people around them—friends, family, and strangers. All must participate in the addiction. Not only that, but consider the medical cost, the time lost to companies, and the loss of money needed for more important things. And worst, a shortened life and perhaps premature death caused by the habit.

Indifference is like smoking. Indifference is a personal choice, but has subtle consequences.

Is indifference a form of rebellion from society, the demands of the world, from God, from religion? Is indifference a conscious or unconscious matter? Is it ever or even thought about? If a person is indifferent does he or she know it? Is it a deliberate choice?

Indifference to God is a fatal mistake. Somewhere along the line we must have made a conscious and deliberate choice not to consider God important in our lives. There are enough evidences that speak of God—whether through nature, "the church bells ringing on a Sunday morn," the visible signs of spiritual significance, or the faith of our friends and relatives. To ignore those is a personal choice.

Remember the movie *Groundhog Day*? The repeated day-in and day-out routine made that movie so appealing. The message of the movie should have a real impact on our living. The main character, Phil Conners, was a weather forecaster from Pittsburgh, covering Groundhog Day for the station in Punxsutawney, Pennsylvania. On their way back to Pittsburgh the news team was forced to turn back because of a snowstorm. They returned to Punxsutawney to stay the night before heading back to Pittsburgh the following day. But when Phil awoke the next morning, it was Groundhog Day all over again. The same happened the next morning, and the next, and the next. Just as he woke every morning faced with the same events—weather forecasting, eating, sleeping, social interactions—he had déjà vu. Bill Murray, the actor who played the character, soon realized that each day was an opportunity to make a difference in his life and others. Every day was the same day yet opportunity and repetition molded and changed him; he viewed circumstances and people differently and took opportunity to make each day better.

We do the same routine ourselves. Our days are virtually the same. We wake, eat, travel, have the same social interactions, and work. But in those repetitions of life, opportunities abound to make a significant difference in ourselves and others.

For many of us, routine seems to be part of the root of indifference, whereas the same routine should give rise to opportunities to vary routine: to be more polite, learn the piano, be more friendly to the same people you meet everyday, broaden your horizons by reading, listen to audio books, observe the world around you, find ways to be nice in uncommon ways.

It is then our choice to do the same dull routine and aid our indifference, or choose to make life exciting.

The church has the indifference problem also. How can we sit in church Sunday after Sunday, year after year and not be affected by the messages that come to us? That certainly is choosing: choosing not to listen, choosing not to change, choosing not to learn, and choosing to be indifferent. Is not hearing or not listening a choice? Indifference? Is it really not listening, or is it a purposeful shutout of the conscious mind? And is not indifference a purposeful shutout to the world around us? We process information by listening and participating, but the shutout mind occurs when we choose not to have it affect us, or change us, or improve us.

The Christian, above all others, should not be labeled indifferent. We have the greater burden (or opportunity, if you will), to be responsible, concerned citizens, stewards, opportunists, evangelists, workers in the kingdom, and doers of good. We have been given much; besides, we have the keys to the kingdom.

When I was in the United States Navy and in basic training, there was a huge sign on the wall of the barracks that read, "I have not been told is no excuse." If then, "I have not been told…" is not an excuse, then how does one become conscious of any act or any situation? That statement would imply a responsibility to every aspect of our lives. But how is that possible without our knowing or ever having knowledge of what we should know? What responsibility is placed on us for not knowing? Is, then, not knowing not seeing? And is not seeing a choice? If that is the premise, then we have a responsibility to every fraction of knowledge out there. Can we be ignorant without responsibility attached to it? Does choice come into play in every aspect of our lives?

In the cartoon "Dilbert" by Scott Adams, Dilbert's boss says, "I can't give you a raise because your project is behind schedule." Dilbert replies, "That's because the vendor delivered defective equipment." His boss replies, "It is your job to anticipate that sort of problem and head it off." "It isn't possible to anticipate and head off every improbable event," Dilbert remarks.

The barracks phrase may be appropriate in the military where much is expected and much required, but in the broad scope of life, we can't be expected to be responsible for everything we don't know—or even everything we do know.

We can't! It is humanly impossible to be responsible for everything that might affect us, but we can be alert to many of the dangers that confront us. Society is filled with advice to protect us: wear your seat belt, smoking may be hazardous to your health, do not drink and drive, wear your seat belt, say no to drugs, do not talk to strangers, lock your doors.

There are many reasons for the causes of indifference and the results and consequences are many: the decline in morality, the breakup of the traditional family unit, the sanctity of life, the search for materialism, and our busyness, to name a few.

Indifference has been predicted from biblical times as recorded in the book of 2 Timothy 3:1 (KJV):

> This know, also, that in the last days perilous times shall come. For men shall be lovers of their own selves, covetous, boasters, proud, blasphemers, disobedient to parents, unthankful, unholy, without natural affection, trucebreakers, false accusers, incontinent, fierce, despisers of those who are good, traitors, heady, high-minded, lovers of pleasures more than lovers of God, having a form of godliness, but denying the power of it; from such turn away…ever learning, and never able to come to the knowledge of the truth.

We don't want to be unduly pessimistic here, but the observance of our culture reveals the biblical prophecy is playing out in modern times. Many people are rude, impatient, careless, pushy, aggressive, impolite, ill-mannered, inconsiderate, and obstinate. Many kids are disrespectful to others and to their own parents. Many parents are self-absorbed in materialism and superficial realities.

Our culture gets diluted into the general mix of "everyone is doing it." That's the indifference problem. Everybody is doing the same thing: watching the same boring TV, following celebrities, commuting, working, stagnating, not creating, not inventing, not reading. Let's break out of that choosing-to-be-indifferent mentality and be individual and proactive, and get involved in the doing. Speaking of which, in "The Doing" chapter, there is a list of things that we can choose that might motivate us to action.

CHAPTER 4

CHOICE AND PRIORITY

Things that matter most must never be at the mercy of the things which matter least.

—Goethe

GET YOUR PRIORITIES straight. How many times have we heard that one? The circumstances of life can and do often waylay us in other directions and distract us from our purpose. Sure life overwhelms and desensitizes us from a variety of sources: the media, life, responsibilities, the small stuff, crises, and demands from parents, employers, and family. Couple those demands with our own mission, purpose, desires, wants, needs, self-fulfillment, and self-actualization, and we have a genuine struggle on our hands.

Suppose we want to be a writer but don't write. Suppose we want an education but can't further our schooling for whatever reason. Suppose we want to lose weight, get in shape, play that guitar, but we don't. We want to spend more time with our children, but don't. Carl Ally, an infamous New York Advertisement Executive once said, "Either you let your life slip away by not doing the things you want to do, or you get up and do them."

It is surely a choice to not do the things we have talent for, the things we want to do, and things we ought to do. I get letters in the mail requesting I give to a certain worthwhile cause to sustain them and enable them to serve their constituents better. I generally throw them away. It is not that I don't care about good causes—sure I do. Am I indifferent? No! Is it a priority for me? No! This one above all other priorities? No! I am really not indifferent to the need, only among the priorities of my benevolence; this one is not high on my giving list. If I had the resources, I would give to them all. We have a needy world, we respond as best we can.

Do we feel guilty over the need and not responding? Yes, sometimes, especially when we read the verse from the New Testament book of James where it says, "Anyone, then, who knows the good he ought to do and doesn't do it, sins."

That verse, taken to heart and to extreme, can overwhelm us with guilt. At some point we have to prioritize our time, energy, and money and pick and choose our benevolence. Generally though, we can adopt John Wesley's philosophy toward our fellow humans:

> *Do all the good you can,*
> *By all the means you can,*
> *In all the ways you can,*
> *At all the times you can,*
> *To all the people you can,*
> *As long as ever you can.*

The busyness in our lives that breeds indifference make us focus on the unimportant and insignificant to the sacrifice of the important. The day-to-day culture of Americans is a life of rushing to and fro from every waking moment to the time one lays his head down at night. The space in between is craziness. Technology has done wonders for our convenience, but has enabled us to cram many more things into a day. We have computers, palm-pilots, appliances, automobiles with GPS aids on board, cell phones, email to instantly keep in touch, text-messaging and many other gadgets that supposedly give us an added quality of life, but they have literally overwhelmed us. In addition, we pack long commutes into our workday coupled with ten to twelve hour days and the evenings are crammed with fast meals, scrambling to get the kids to events and…whew! It even makes me tired writing about it.

The downside of all this activity is we are further desensitized to creativity, family gatherings, friendly conversations, letter writing, meditation, worship, time alone, healthy lifestyle habits, and reading. It is not that the things we do are unimportant, they are, but a society that constantly feeds this frenzy day in and day out leads itself to unhealthiness, tiredness, depression, mental instability, stress, heart problems, and other physical and psychological problems.

It is no accident that God built into the cycle of life six days of work and one day of rest. Rest is important in the recovery of the mind and body. Balance and moderation are the keys to healthy living.

CHAPTER 5

CHOOSING TO BE WILLFULLY IGNORANT

THIS IS AN unusual one—to be ignorant by choice. Actually it is ignorance by deliberate commission rather than unconscious omission. It is an act of choosing not to know. That is different from indifference. Realistically, we can't know everything—we don't want to know everything—but there are things we should know that might be very valuable to our well-being.

The willfully ignorant group has an antonym: the unwillfully ignorant. They are ignorant by lack of opportunity. There are approximately one billion people (20%) in the world who are illiterate and without cultured knowledge. Out of that billion, the majority live in developing countries where poverty or political regimes have made it virtually impossible for them to get the basic necessities of life like food, shelter, and security. Life opportunities such as education are even further from reality.

Hardly anyone could read or write in medieval times. They were not ignorant in the sense that they were helpless. They had jobs or a trade, but they were just unlearned and unskilled in terms of being literate. Schooling or literacy was relegated to a few: aristocrats, families of nobility, or the religious hierarchy. The peasants and commoners were under subjection and authority of the elite. Literacy for the most part was discouraged for the common people. Education might mean thought, making decisions for one's self and perhaps lead to unrest; and that was a perceived threat to the people of power.

Yet today, we have an approximate 53% high school drop-out rate and the kids who reach adulthood are hardly literate.

In his book *The Closing of the American Mind*, Allan Bloom states in referring to the contemporary pop music…

> My concern here is not with the moral effects of this music—whether it leads to sex, violence or drugs. The issue here is its effect on education, and I believe it ruins the imagination of young people and makes it very difficult for them to have a passionate relationship to the art and thought that are the substance of liberal education. The first sensuous experiences are decisive in determining the taste for the whole of life, and they are the link between the animal and spiritual in us…. Education is not sermonizing to children against their instincts and pleasures, but providing a natural continuity between what they feel and what they can and should be. But this is a lost art. (Pgs.79, 80)

There may be a fine line between being indifferent, apathetic, don't care or just not interested, but we are expressly concerned with ignorance as a deliberate choice. For instance, I choose to not know anything about nutrition, about the universe, about investing, about preparing for the end of life. Granted there are many things that go on in life that we could just as easily not care about and that's fine. Sometimes, however, the irony here is that some things do pertain—to me and everybody else. For not knowing may be the difference between health and ill health, the quality of life or life and death.

This chapter doesn't necessarily focus on a health issue, but it is a good example as health is a nationwide crisis with obesity, high cholesterol, heart disease, and diabetes on the up rise. We take such pleasure in eating not only because it is necessary, but actively seek food as one of the pleasures of life. Because Americans enjoy our food abundance to excess, we are literally eating our way to ill health and even premature death.

In an effort to educate the public, the Food and Drug Administration has encouraged food suppliers to post the nutrition facts on each product being sold. The food pyramid is published on many products to guide and suggest our proper food habits. Almost at every word, quality of life includes the value of proper eating habits, exercise, and sufficient rest. To be unaware of those important messages is purposeful ignorance. It should be our responsibility to educate ourselves and apply that knowledge for our health benefit. Yet most continue to be nutritionally ignorant.

In his book *What You Don't Know May Be Killing You!* Dr. Don Colbert states that "most sickness is self-inflicted—either by willful destructive habits or by ignorance… because the average person doesn't have a clue about basic health and nutrition." (pgs. 2,4)

Food and its consequences is just one of the many areas of life that has potential hazards if we choose to be ignorant of them. Nutrition was a good example, but there are a myriad of things that can waylay us by our willful ignorance. They are different for different people but a few can be listed: drugs, smoking, poor automobile maintenance, ignoring safety issues in the home and the workplace, and our ignorance of our spiritual well-being.

I know people who are willfully ignorant. They just choose to not know, and seemingly to not know anything. Choosing to not know for them is a comfortable habit.

The irony of this scenario is that these individuals are content. They are not driven by the need to know more and more or the need to know the news or the weather, but are simply content to eat, be healthy, bask in the affection of family, and accept life as it is. In many ways that mind-set is not without worthy consideration.

In the area of our religious and spiritual condition, there is a big difference between indifference and being willfully ignorant. Here ignorance is the greater sin.

Biblically speaking, God won't let us be ignorant of our responsibilities as human beings. There are certain requirements He demands. Take for instance Micah 6:8 where He clearly lays out what is required of humankind. "He has showed you, O man, what is good. And what does the Lord require of you? To act justly and to love mercy and to walk humbly with your God." (KJV). Three things He requires: do right (act justly), show love, be compassionate, be kind (love mercy) and love the Lord with all your heart, mind, and soul (walk humbly with your God).

We can say we know nothing about this responsibility, or if we do, we can ignore it, be indifferent about it, or be willfully ignorant by not wanting to know. Does that excuse the requirement? Let's go back to the statement, "I have not been told is no excuse."

Let's examine further this willfully ignorant scenario.

God's relationship with Israel, the Hebrew nation of His chosen people, is characterized in a story in the Old Testament book of Hosea. In Hosea 4: 6, the Israelites are branded as being willfully ignorant of God's requirements of them. "My people are destroyed from lack of knowledge. Because you have rejected knowledge, I also reject you as my priests; because you have ignored the law of your God, I will also ignore your children."

The consequences of not knowing or being willfully ignorant is sometimes lifestyle threatening.

I don't believe that under the guise of Christianity or a godly created member of the human race that we can be totally ignorant of who God is, or what our moral responsibility is to our fellow humans. We can be illiterate, uneducated, and socially unaware, but cannot come to the end of life and to the judgment and say, "I was not told about God…"

> " since what may be known about God is plain to them, because God had made it plain to them. For since the creation of the world God's invisible qualities—his eternal power and divine nature—have been clearly seen, being understood from what had been made, so that men are without excuse."
>
> —Romans 1:19-20

The evidence is clear. We have to be willing to see it and not closed to objectivity. "The heavens declare the glory of God; the skies proclaim the work of his hands. Day after day they pour forth speech; night after night they display knowledge" (Psalm 19:1-2).

How is it that we see but do not see, hear but do not hear, have learning but are not able to come to the knowledge of the truth? Are we willfully and spiritually blinded by the "father of lies," by our own choices, or has God withdrawn His spirit from us? By whatever reason for our lack of godly knowledge, we chose it. We can blame no one.

God commissioned Isaiah, His prophet, to

"Go tell the Israelites His message: *Be ever hearing, but never understanding; be ever seeing, but never perceiving. Make the heart of this people calloused; make their ears dull and close their eyes. Otherwise they might see with their eyes, hear with their ears, understand with their hearts, and turn and be healed.*

—Isaiah 6: 9-10

This was a prophecy about the people of Israel. They could hear but wouldn't, could see but chose not to, could understand, but refused. That is willful ignorance. It could also be a prophecy about us.

CHAPTER 6

LIFE AND DEATH CHOICES

Greater love has no one than this, that he lay down his life for his friends.

—John 15:13

O N THE MORNING of September 11, 2001, the passengers of flight 93 made a choice. They stormed the cockpit where terrorists had seized control of Flight 93. Those brave souls forced the crashing of the plane in a field outside Shanksville, Pennsylvania. The people made the ultimate sacrifice to save unnumbered people from harm as Flight 93 was believed to be headed toward the White House in Washington, D.C.

People make choices every day to save others without regard for their own safety or endangerment. For some it is a chosen lifestyle or occupation: firemen, police, rescue, military, National Guard. Sometimes willing individuals choose to give their lives to save many. As in the case of Fight 93, those are true heroes.

The sanctity of life is important. Life is precious. It is sacred. It is God given.

There is a societal inclination to degrade human life as less sacred due to cultural and media influence. Common talk of the issues of the day like abortion, euthanasia, assisted suicide, and life support tend to numb us toward the importance of sanctity of life. There is a great debate, with some, whether life starts at conception or later. Issues about the day-after pill, abortion, and partial birth extraction are common news today and fall into the pro-life pro-choice camps. The resulting ethical and moral dilemma is a source of societal and political strife and seemingly has no clear answers.

Further, with world population increasing, food and water shortages, burdening of the elderly, and no jobs, will society begin to think of euthanasia, genocide, infanticide, assisted suicide, assisted termination of life as the norm rather than the exception? How will we then put value on life?

Harm's Way

We don't really deliberately choose for ourselves a life of danger, although there are many occupations and circumstances that put us in harm's way. Some we have control over, some we don't. There are occupations like firemen, policemen, the military (especially during wartime), construction workers, miners, the FBI, and CIA to name a few, who voluntarily put their lives on the line every day. And there are sports-related activities that put individuals in harm's way: mountain climbers, skydivers, bungee jumpers, football, boxing, soccer. Some of these life events automatically put us into situations that might result in life-threatening or bodily harm situations. Generally we should not intentionally put ourselves in situations that affect our life or health. Some that come to mind are: drug use and abuse, drinking and driving, unsafe work practices, unsafe home environment, intentionally being in places that foster violence, sports activities without proper padding/safety measures, homes without adequate detecting devices (smoke, carbon monoxide), poor driving habits, and a host of others.

The above listing is mostly aimed at occupations and sports and related activities that might be harmful to our well being. There are, however, other habits, traits, or cultural activities that fall under the category of being potentially harmful. Don't put yourself in situations that might lead to arrest: bad credit, bankruptcy, social impropriety, theft (stealing, shoplifting), spousal abuse, sexual issues such as date rape, corruption of a minor or insurance fraud, to name just a few.

At a more day-to-day level, our choices have life and death implications: running red lights, aggressive driving, smoking, driving under the influence of alcohol, taking unnecessary chances, putting ourselves at risk, not utilizing safety measures, (fire prevention, helmets, safety belts, first aid education, and others). Making proper health and safety choices and exercising them is a life-saving imperative for our well-being, our home, our car.

Cars are a particular source of danger. With 100 million households that have an average of two cars per family, no wonder there are accidents that take lives, destroy property, and cost the country millions of dollars in damage and insurance.

According to Car-Accidents.com, 6,420,000 auto accidents occurred in the US in the year 2005. There were 2.9 million people injured and 42,636 people killed. That is one death every 13 minutes. And worldwide? One point three million people are killed each year.

How can those statistics be lowered? Drive safely, use seat belts, slow down, and don't drink and drive.

Drugs

Modern medicine has been a God-given blessing to mankind. Through the various discoveries of the likes of penicillin, vaccines, and other disease preventative medicines, most killer diseases have been virtually eradicated in our contemporary society. Drugs, as well, do wonders in alleviating pain, curing afflictions, and making life a little easier.

Most drugs have side effects and if not taken under the guidance of a physician, can become habit forming, addictive and abused by choice. Taken to extreme, drugs can take over our lives.

A word about semantics. Addiction is a word that has many connotations, but today is generally thought to be negative. Addictions can be good. We can be addicted to love, or golf, or football, food, reading, or family. However, presently in this writing, addiction is inferred to be a bad, life altering, no-choice phenomenon.

Jeffrey Schaler, in his book *Addiction Is a Choice*, describes addiction as one's individual choice. If we choose to be addicted to golf or drugs then it is our decision. Drugs certainly can be destructive, but the choice is ours to make. He says, "the price of freedom is a free society is responsibility for the consequences of one's actions. Liberty and responsibility are positively correlated. That's a fact. People who claim addiction causes people to smoke say the two are negatively correlated.

That's fiction. We cannot increase freedom by decreasing personal responsibility. That's the road to serfdom." (pg. 60)

We all dabble in drugs to some extent whether it be caffeine (coffee, tea, sodas), tobacco, (smoking, chewing, snuff), social alcohol, (wine, beer, hard spirits), pain relievers (aspirin, ibuprofen, acetaminophen related products), sleep aids, and other over-the-counter drugs. We may not classify these as addictive substances, but they are listed in any drug publication as a physiological and/or psychological drug that our bodies and mind need, want, or require. All have side effects. Some of these are addictive to some degree, but socially accepted. We feel these are innocent enough yet have withdrawal consequences—some mild (headaches, jitters) and others—like street drugs, alcohol, and tobacco—can lead to hardened addiction, yet they, too, can be reduced or abstained by choice until such time they take our choices and will to withdraw.

While alcohol in its many forms is not illegal except for young people under 21, it remains the nation's number one drug of choice and can lead to serious life-altering addiction when taken to extreme.

Tobacco also is one of the nation's most habit-forming drugs and restricted only to minors. The legal age to buy tobacco products is 18 in 46 out of the 50 US states, and age 19 in Alabama, Alaska, New Jersey, and Utah.

Tobacco use in the United States kills more people than AIDS, homicides, drugs, fires, and auto accidents combined. Translated, one out of every five deaths is attributed to tobacco use. (www.resolvequitsmoking.com) And, oddly enough, tobacco use is inversely proportional to income and educational level. The greater use is attributed to the poor and uneducated.

Even over-the-counter or prescription drugs, which we may take on our own or prescribed to us by our doctor, may be habit forming and become addictive. There is a frightening trend among teens today to use over-the-counter drugs as so-called recreational drugs to get a "high." Dextromethorphan-based cough medicines are the "high" of choice. Hardened addicts will take anything for a fix: dextromethorphan-based drugs found mostly in cough syrup, Nyquil, mouthwash, and anything else perceived to be a possible "high." We as drug takers and doctors as drug prescribers have to be careful of the potential addictive traits in the medicines. The public has to be proactive in the use and selection of over-the-counter and prescribed medicines. Don't ingest drugs lightly or without valid research.

Those many drugs classified as illegal substances: cocaine, amphetamines, methamphetamines, hallucinogens (LSD), marijuana (which approximately 12 million Americans partake of) can and does lead to addiction and dependency.

Mind-altering drugs strip a person of all personal choices. He or she may be beyond making rational decisions and it takes concerned friends and family to get sons, daughters, wives, and husbands to a drug-rehabilitation program. If they cannot or will not consent to rehabilitation, they have to be forcibly removed by transporters—individuals who are contracted to "kidnap" or forcibly remove the person with the family's permission.

"By definition, an addiction offers no choice to the addict and often is the direct cause of serious disruption in the person's health or life-style. The most serious addictions of all involve psychoactive drugs. These substances radically alter the user's mind and body, undermining health, economic stability, and social functioning; it is this form of addiction and abuse that most immediately threatens all of society" (*Substance Abuse Prevention and Treatment,* page 37 Avraham, Regina, 1988, Chelsea House Publishers).

There are day-to-day real-life stories that play out across the nation. People struggle to get family and friends into a rehab program. Some eventually will go but many will not. The power of drug use is overwhelming. Whether drugs, alcohol, gambling, or smoking, the power of addiction exceeds persuasion and choice.

Of the estimated 22 million individuals who need drug rehabilitation, only a fraction actually enter a program, and of that fraction, only another small number actually are rehabilitated. (Article by Jason Gluckman http://ezinearticles.com)

Taking drugs of any kind is a person's choice. Becoming a drug addict is also a person's choice. However, and this is a big however, serious addiction and certain drugs will strip one's power to choose.

CHAPTER 7

CHOICES THAT PROMOTE HEALTHY LIVING

WHEN WE LIVE a lifestyle that promotes health and happiness, we are much better off in life than otherwise.

A healthful lifestyle is more than dieting, watching one's weight, or being in shape. It is a lifelong endeavor to foster a healthy mind, spirit, and body in the environment surrounding the home, car, and workplace.

The Nutrition Research Newsletter (April 2005) says: "Chronic diseases are responsible for most deaths in the United States. Approximately 70-90% of these deaths are estimated to be caused by poor nutrition, sedentary living and tobacco use and are largely preventable. The greatest improvements in physical health in the United States will be made by helping individuals adopt and maintain more healthful lifestyles."

What are our choices that would foster a lifestyle?

- Sleeping well is a physical necessity, but more than that is a regeneration of the bodily functions. On the average, seven to ten hours, (dependent on age), are necessary to restore and rest our bodies from the stress of everyday life.
- Find the right mate. That one decision will determine your life-long happiness or misery. Compatibility is more than physical attraction; it is about mutual interests, intellectual stimulation, similar likes, mutual respect, and above all, love.

- Find a way to do what we like and make a living at it. We all have talents and interests. Would it be better to work at something we like to do instead of making a living because we need money?
- Finding comfort in God is a sure way to have peace of mind and a clear conscience amidst stressful lives.
- Eliminate habits that prevent good health: smoking, drug use, alcohol. These are covered extensively in chapter 6, but to reiterate here, these three labeled vices are hazardous to our well-being if taken to extreme.
- Moderation in all things as Benjamin Franklin would say, and taken to heart, it is the best advice for a healthy life that eliminates extremes: overeating, overuse of drugs.
- Eat a balanced diet, including five servings of fruits and vegetables each day.
- Exercising regularly is a proven benefit to relieve stress, improve overall health, and keep our weight under control.
- Practice safety habits at home to prevent falls and fractures and prevent life threatening harm. As most accidents occur at home, it makes sense to focus our attention on those unsafe potentials. Install smoke and carbon monoxide detectors, put locks on doors, keep debris away from steps or underfoot, install hand rails, child proof your home, avoid sharp edges (buy soft or rounded furniture), when climbing use appropriate climbing devices, put chemicals in a safe place and away from children; store guns in a locked cabinet or away from access by children, always insist on helmets for bike riders, skateboarders, and for other potential head trauma activities.
- Always wear a seat belt. Always. Secure children as recommended by car seat manufacturers.
- Stay in contact with family and friends. Frequent contact with friends and relatives will assure safe living.
- Avoid overexposure to the sun and cold. Dress appropriately. Always carry or wear a jacket when it's cold and always have a hat, sunscreen, or cover-up for when you are caught unexpectedly in sunlight. Wear sunglasses with UV protection to protect eyesight.

- Keep personal and financial life in order. Avoid credit card debt. Prepare a grab-and-go kit that has the essentials should you need to vacate your home quickly. Secure important papers, such as wills, insurance policies, birth certificates, etc., in a safety deposit box.
- Have a positive attitude toward life. Do things that make you happy. Avoid angry and abrasive people.
- Avoid crime, immorality, evil practices. Don't put yourself in harm's way—those situations that might cause harm or injury or death. Most of all, don't allow yourself to be caught up in situations that lead to jail time. Here is a statistic that sobers us. There were, according to the Wrongful Death Institute, as of June of 2003, 2,078,570 individuals incarcerated for crimes committed. Some are less serious with short-term commitments whereas others are long-term or lifers. Jail is not a nice place. It not only labels you for life as a criminal or a sexual predator, but it is hazardous to one's mental and bodily health. It is life threatening and demeaning.
- Treat all people with respect and consideration. Treat others like you want to be treated.

The interconnectedness of the body, spirit, and mind is a cohabitation that can't be neglected. A balanced existence is ideal where our body is nurtured, our mind is stimulated and educated, and the spiritual life is fed with positive godly influences. The absence of any one of these is a life out of balance.

CHAPTER 8

CHOICES AND BLAME

Up to a point a man's life is shaped by environment, heredity, movements and changes in the world about him. Then there comes a time when it lies within his grasp to shape the clay of his life into the sort of thing he wishes to be. Only the weak blame parents, their race, their times, lack of good fortune, or the quirks of fate. Everyone has within his power to say, this I am today, that I will be tomorrow.

—Louis L'Amour

WE LIVE IN an unaccountable culture with seemingly no responsibility for our own actions. That mentality is prevalent throughout our society—in children, parents, corporate leadership, and even invading our highest levels government.

We often place blame rather than take responsibility for our choices and resulting actions and consequences. We tend not to admit when wrong or when unpleasant choices are made. Taking responsibility for our actions is difficult; we don't want to admit our faults, mistakes, and wrong decisions. Some excuses are, "I wasn't told," "I never had the opportunity," "everybody is doing it," "it's not my fault," "they owe it to me," "they don't treat me right," "they don't like me."

It's easy to place blame and circumvent our own inadequacies. We think it excuses us. And in some remote way we may even believe that it is not really our fault; but that something or someone is causing our dismay: society, lack of opportunity, circumstances, and destiny. That may be true in certain circumstances, but mostly we are products of our own making. We reap what we sow. There is really no one to blame but ourselves.

Biblically, there are instances where characters tried to divert blame from themselves to another person or circumstance. Two examples come to mind: one goes back to the story of Adam and Eve in the garden where God strictly forbade eating the fruit of or even touching the Tree of Knowledge of good and evil. The serpent intervened by saying that they would not surely die but would be like gods.

Seeing that the tree was pleasant to look at and the fruit appealing, they ate. Immediately their eyes were open and saw their nakedness and hid themselves. God asked them what they had done, and Adam said "this woman gave me the fruit I ate it." When God asked Eve, "what have you done?" Eve said "the serpent beguiled me."

The other story is of Peter and the account is from the Gospel of Mark, 14: 27-31, 66-72. The scene takes place on the Mount of Olives.

> When they had sung a hymn, they went out to the Mount of Olives. "You will all fall away," Jesus told them, "for it is written: "'I will strike the shepherd, and the sheep will be scattered.'

> "But after I have risen, I will go ahead of you into Galilee." Peter declared, "Even if all fall away, I will not." "I tell you the truth," Jesus answered, "today—yes tonight—before the rooster crows twice you yourself will disown me three times." But Peter insisted emphatically, "Even if I have to die with you, I will never disown you."

> While Peter was below in the courtyard, one of the servant girls of the high priest came by. When she saw Peter warming himself, she looked closely at him. "You also are with that Nazarene, Jesus, "she said. But he denied it. "I don't know or understand what you're talking about," he said, and went out into the entryway.

> When the servant girl saw him there, she said again to those standing around, "This fellow is one of them." Again he denied it.

After a little while, those standing near said to Peter, "Surely you are one of them, for you are a Galilean."

He began to call down curses on himself, and he swore to them, "I don't know this man you're talking about"

Immediately the rooster crowed the second time. Then Peter remembered the word Jesus had spoken to him: "Before the rooster crows twice you will disown me three times." And he broke down and wept.

In these two biblical examples, Adam, Eve, and Peter did not take responsibility for their actions and placed blame on others, circumstances, or just plain lied. The consequences for the early garden keepers were enormous for them and for the rest of humanity. The consequences for Peter were broken promises, personal failure, and denying God. These are lessons for all of us.

Dale Carnegie, in his book *How to Win Friends & Influence People,* says as an axiom, "If you are wrong, admit it quickly and emphatically." He goes on to say, "When we are right, let's try to win people gently and tactfully to our way of thinking, and when we are wrong—and that will be surprisingly often, if we are honest with ourselves—let's admit our mistakes quickly and with enthusiasm. Not only will that technique produce astonishing results; but, believe it or not, it is a lot more fun, under the circumstances, than trying to defend oneself."

If we can come to the realization that life is really in our control and that we are the ones that navigate our direction, we can start to take responsibility for every aspect of our lives. It is too difficult to correct all the ills of the world, all the causes that affect us, all the evils that try and undermine us, but knowing that we are in control of our own destiny is not necessarily easy but infinitely easier than correcting those things out of our control.

Reinhold Niebuhr wrote this often-quoted saying: "God grant me the serenity to accept the things I cannot change; the courage to change the things I can; and the wisdom to know the difference."

Sometimes, however, due to accidents, death, sickness, and disease we place blame on the circumstances of life, people, situations, governments, and even God. We feel better if we place blame, but often there is no one or nothing at fault, it's just life.

Blame, anger, and bitterness have taken many lives. Not in the sense of loss of life, but in the sense of being stripped of peace, contentment, and a conscience-free existence. Everyone deserves peace.

CHAPTER 9

PROMISES AND CHOICE

W E HAVE RESPONSIBILITY in all sorts of life's dealings: school, parents, our marriage, employer, our government, our fellow man, children, ourselves, and our God.

One of the most disturbing facts of our present-day culture is there is a growing trend toward ignoring responsibility and breaking our sacred word. We are in a culture that places blame on circumstances, parents, society, our plight, or anything else that will minimize our own faults and obligations. We think we are not accountable to anyone.

There was a time when a person's word was as binding and honorable as a written contract. Now we have to put each other in binding agreements with penalties if broken. There are even nuptial agreements that obligate a couple financially if the marriage vows fail. Any failure in contract or agreement might result in a legal suit and court proceedings. As a result, the United States is the most sue-conscious country on the planet.

We have responsibility based upon our relationships, our promises, our contracts. We obey our parents because they have authority over us, but more than that, it is respect, honor, and relationship. It is one of the Ten Commandments. "Honor thy father and mother for your days shall be long upon the earth." It is not only a commandment, but a promise. That is how important our parental relationship is. We obey the laws of the land that are instituted for our well-being. We honor our contracts, (house mortgage, car payment, credit card debt) because we said we would, but also the penalties are severe. We fulfill our employment obligation as the employer pays us for service and expects value from his investment. We fulfill our marriage vows because we promised. We fulfill our obligation to our church membership because we said we would. All of these aren't volunteer agreements to be treated lightly; they are moral, spiritual, and often legally binding.

We can't divorce wives or husbands just because we don't feel like being married anymore; we stay the course because we have promised to love, comfort, honor, and keep him or her for better or worse, for richer or poorer, in sickness and in health. And, forsaking all others, we promise to be faithful only to him or her so long as we both shall live. Is that unduly confining? Many think so as the divorce rate is running at about a 40% to 50% marriage failure.

We can't renege on our responsibilities just because we don't feel like it. It is not about feeling, it is about enduring. It is about character: honesty, faithfulness, integrity.

God asks us to be faithful in all things. He would not require and command us to keep His promises and covenants if they weren't enduring. Enduring is a biblical teaching.

Multiple times, Scripture declares that God promises to uphold His covenants and be the enduring security for His creation. After all, in spite of our faults, our broken promises, our sins, He still reaches out to save His people by the death of that perfect sacrifice—Jesus Christ.

The promises of God are many:

All men are like grass,
And all their glory is like the flowers of the field;
The grass withers and the flowers fall,
But the word of the Lord stands forever.

—1 Peter 1: 25

Jesus Christ is the same yesterday and today and forever.

—Hebrews 13:8

Whether by contract, a handshake, a verbal promise, a vow, a pledge, a work responsibility, a membership, or covenant, we have the responsibility to stay the course. It has to be that way. If breaking is the norm, then what is sacred? We could just do as we please without accountability to anyone or anything.

Obeying our responsibility is our God-commanded charge. He demands perfection from us and demands our whole being. "If you love me you will keep my commandments," Jesus said.

CHAPTER 10

CHOOSING TO PARENT

THE TRADITIONAL FAMILY unit consisting of a husband, wife, and children no longer seems adequate to describe the various households we see in today's society. There are nuclear, blended, binuclear, same-sex arrangements, foster, and single parents. Many individuals of these combinations choose to parent. Grandparents who may not choose to parent suddenly find themselves caretakers of their grandchildren. Whatever arrangement individuals desire to have or raise children, parents then not only have the responsibility of bearing, raising, and nurturing children, but also to provide the basic necessities of life: food, shelter, education, social concerns, medical support, and establishing quality of life; and also the awesome responsibility of being a mentor, friend, supporter, spiritual advisor, and educator. It is a lifelong endeavor.

Then there are individuals who choose not to be parents and don't want to be, but by whatever circumstance, find themselves with child. These are the unwanted children who are either aborted or brought into this world under the most undesirable of circumstances. According to Janice Shaw Crouse, Ph.D. of the Beverly LaHaye Institute, "The facts are that six million American women become pregnant every year—half of them are unmarried. Of those three million unmarried pregnant women, almost half have an abortion and approximately the other half become single mothers. Very few of the unmarried pregnant

women marry the father of their child or give the child up for adoption."
Why is this? There are no accidents where children are concerned.
The mechanics are obvious and prevention obvious. Having children,
whether on purpose, by so-called "accidents," or from passion requires
obligation, responsibility, and lifelong commitment.

As far as choice is concerned, just the decision to have children
and raise them and nurture them is an endeavor not to be entered into
lightly. Can we provide for them, educate them, be a full-time caretaker,
support their needs, and provide a loving and caring home life?

Today's parents have a job on their hands. There is no course on
parenting. Parents are cast out in society to struggle for themselves
without knowledge, skills, or being properly armed for the challenge of
raising children. I have observed three or four generations of families
over my years of life and see the shift in the parenting culture from
the forties to the new millennium. I realize parents today need to
have a more hands-on approach to foster good families. Why today
over any other generation? The cultural demands: the opportunities,
the distractions, the temptations of society (drugs, violence, sex, peer
pressure, materialism) impact parents much more than when I was raised
in the 1940s. How can parents muster the knowledge required to give
children what they need? How do we supervise proper eating habits
when TV is marketing a fat and sugar lifestyle? How can we limit or
restrict the artificial violence they see on TV and video games? How can
we provide hands-on living experiences rather than a world of virtual
reality? Kids are loosing touch with the world. Parents must screen kids
from the world of television, video games, and the internet and replace
it with challenging, educational and world experiences. Schools teach
kids about life but parents must teach kids how to live. How can we sift
through the myriad of demands on kids these days and yet allow them
their childhood and normal growth experiences? All these and more
confront today's parents.

It is just as important as ever to provide children with a Christian
foundation. With distractions abounding, it is easy to ignore the
important formation of the arts, religious teachings, and plain living.
Again we might ask the question, is spirituality important in one's life?
Is a strong moral foundation necessary for social survival? Which would

we rather consider important when confronted with a difficult situation, a person with moral values or one without?

To reiterate, who teaches morality today? Not our educational systems, not television, not video games, not the street or our friends or our peers. Who then? It falls to parents. It not only falls to parents, it is their job.

This is a deliberate choice for parents. Parents must ensure that children get a moral foundation and Christian principles. There can be no greater work for parents than to lead and direct their children in the ways of God. This is a decision parents must make for them. Kids follow examples. If religion and church attendance aren't important to parents, they won't be for the kids. Parental example is a powerful motivator. Being an example not only pertains to religious values, it carries over into other areas of life as well. If parents smoke, it is likely the kids will follow when given an opportunity. Abusive and angry parents lead kids to be abusive. Alcoholism leads to alcoholism.

It is crucial for parents to equip children with necessary tools to make wise choices. Sure, once raised, kids will make their own decisions and therefore have the responsibility for those choices, but equipping is the parent's job. It is crucial for their well-being, it is crucial for society, and it is crucial for future generations.

CHAPTER 11

CHOOSING VALUES
AND MORALS

W E ALL HAVE values-- those personal ideals that matter to us. Our core values are individual and subjective: like patriotism or honesty or fairness. There are many others that would add up to perhaps a hundred if we really start thinking. Values are important. They are those accepted ideals each of us consider important to regulate our conduct in life and with our fellow men. The Boy Scouts have their own list and know them as their "law": trustworthy, loyal, helpful, friendly, courteous, kind, obedient, cheerful, thrifty, brave, clean, and reverent.

As a nation, core values are equally important. Ideals like democracy, freedom, individual rights, and liberty are at the root of our heritage. They are the binding and enduring forces that make our government unique among the countries of the world.

Holding on to core values is important as a foundation for our ideals, but we must be sensitive to the time and placc where certain ones must be altered, changed, reshaped to be applicable to the moment. We often hold on to values and traditions that become a handicap or even hazardous to our well-being if not changed to meet circumstances.

Jared Diamond, in his book *Collapse,* says that "the other crucial choice illuminated by past [societies] involves the courage to make painful decisions about values. Which of the values that formerly served a society well can continue to be maintained under new changed circumstances?"

As individuals or an organization or religious institution, we may feel reluctant to abandon a policy, a program, or a tradition that we still feel ought to work but doesn't.

The government of Myanmar has an isolationist military government and philosophy where they see themselves as self-sufficient and resistant to outsiders, especially the West. The country, formally Burma, has a poverty-level population of about 47 million. The country also has one of the poorest human rights records of any other country.

When the cyclone struck Myanmar Province in May of 2008, the Myanmar government resisted outside United Nation assistance. They reluctantly accepted air dropped supplies but refused distribution by outsiders. Even though the cyclone devastated the country and initially killed about 100,000 and left another two million homeless, the government still took the isolationist attitude.

Here is a clear example of how a government thinks things ought to work and continue to work among severe circumstances yet is still resistant to change even when the need is evident. In a world that is now "flat," with each country depending upon another for food, fuel, and survival, isolationism is a devastating philosophy.

While values are personal and subjective, morals are more foundational and absolute. They are guidelines to regulate our conduct. For the most part, we all recognize and agree to participate in them as a normal and accepted part of society. Whether that code comes from tradition, parents, religion, church, our own built-in conscience, Boy Scouts, or some other source, we accept responsibility for our actions as they relate to our fellow humans.

Regardless of what our belief system is or even if there isn't any, we all prescribe to a certain moral stability. It has nothing to do with being religious or Christian or saintly, a secular society adheres to a moral code because everyone agrees there is right and wrong, evil and good in the world, and there has to be a temperance and code of conduct. How else could the world be ordered? Otherwise it would be in chaos without any mechanism to temper it.

How do we learn principles of right and wrong? Who teaches values and morality? Do schools? Should they? Is it their mission? Suppose some school students are dishonest, disrespectful, or belligerent, and then whose place is it to correct or instill values? It's already too late when parents or society have failed them. But for many reasons the schools can't teach or correct because morality might be considered a religious discipline. For one, teaching morality is not the schools' mission; two, the separation of church and state issue prevails; and three, students should already have a code of conduct.

If the schools are not doing it and the parents aren't, then who? Does television? No. If anything it teaches otherwise. Granted, television is a medium that produces some educational programming, entertainment, newsworthy information, and religious teaching, but for the most part, television is a mind-numbing and moral deprecating medium.

Do movies teach morality? Generally no, however there are good movies and some are like literature, well worth the watching. Like television, movies contribute to the decline of one's morals through sex, drugs, extra-marital affairs, crime, and behavior unbecoming to proper citizenry.

What about video games? It is entertaining and enhances mind/body coordination, but also certainly teaches violence, disrespect, and crime in certain games. In my mind these games are one of the foremost contributions to the degradation of our youth. Parents need to play a more proactive role in what content these games present to our children.

Do parents provide morality training to children? They should and most do, but society will testify that morality training isn't provided at home. In the parental segment of this book, the content talks about and suggests the importance of good parenting. It includes providing the child with a home free of violence, a supportive environment, and a base for moral training, love, and comfort.

Does society? Society doesn't teach. It will however monitor behavior as in crime prevention, traffic violations, and conduct according to the laws of the land and provide guidance if its citizen are found going astray. But no, it doesn't teach morality.

Who then does? If schools do not, the entertainment industry doesn't, society doesn't, parents don't, then who?

History does. Literature does. The churches do. Religion does.

Isn't our world and our quality of life better if everyone exercised the principles of right, goodness, kindness, and peacefulness? Even if we don't adhere to a strong religious belief system, isn't our world more conducive to social compatibility?

How can we unite the world around this mutual human respect?

When we are moral, we treat others with respect and do not indulge in practices that harm others or ourselves.

We are continuously confronted with moral dilemmas in life: lying, stealing, the treatment of others, oppression, taking life, abortion, euthanasia, and suicide just to name a few. There aren't new moral issues today versus, say, thousands of years ago. People are people and morality, or the lack thereof, is the same today as yesterday. In contemporary culture however, we are confronted with those so-called gray areas that we label as situation ethics—no clear answers of right and wrong.

What is the difference between moral and ethical issues? It would seem the moral ones are the most clear, more identifiable. The Ten Commandments are the moral law: thou shalt not steal, kill, lie, covet, is either clearly religious or socially acceptable conduct. The ethical issues are often the most difficult to sort out.

> *...the issues we now confront were unimaginable to the men who made America. Abortion, bioethics, stem-cell research, euthanasia, the rights of homosexuals, the teaching of the theory of evolution versus creationism or intelligent design—these were not part of the world of the Founders. What light, some say, could the eighteenth century possibly shed on such questions well over two hundred years later? Yet the founders hoped they were constructing a republic that would withstand the vicissitudes of time and chance and would, with amendment, endure. Why else work so hard, think so deeply, argue so closely, and design so carefully a government that would check passions, thus raising the odds that it would serve Americans from age to age?*
>
> —American Gospel, page 246

The clear instruction of the commandment that instructs us "do not kill' is much more difficult to sort out when confronted with the situation of whether to pull life support from a woman who has been brain dead for months or years. Take the Terry Schiavo case. Terri collapsed from a heart attack in 1990 and was revived; however, her brain was oxygen deprived too long and she lived in a comatose state for fifteen years. Terri had normal bodily functions but was unresponsive to external stimuli. There were many efforts on the part of her husband to terminate her life by a "do not resuscitate" order. Yet Terri's parents insisted she be kept alive for a possible miracle recovery. Her husband wanted the courts to terminate her life support. The legal battle ensued for seven of her fifteen years, and then the courts finally gave permission to pull life support.

This scenario has occurred many times with many people. What is the clear answer? Is disconnecting life support murder? Is it inhumane or humane to sustain life with no hope of recovery?

There are many critical issues that face the twenty-first century ethicist. If you think the premature termination of life is murder, then perhaps the Terri Schiavo incident is a murder case. You may think the loving and humane thing is to terminate Terri's life based on medical facts. She will lay in bed until such time as she dies naturally or by some other means. What is the "Christian thing to do," the loving thing, the wrong thing, the humane thing?

What about the many other issues we face today: death wishes, living wills, euthanasia, assisted suicide, cloning, and the explosive issue of abortion?

Without going into the Roe vs. Wade case of 1973 that initiated the Supreme Court's decision allowing women the right for a legal abortion, you, the reader, review the statistics and decide its implication.

According to the Alan Guttmacher Institute, worldwide, there are 46 million abortions per year. In the United States, the court's decision legalized approximately 1.3 million babies to be aborted yearly and the result is 48,589,993 abortions performed since 1973. Would you have wanted to be among that number?

Joseph Fletcher was the one who coined "*situation ethics*" in his book by the same title. In it, he premised that love is the deciding and driving force in a seemingly unsolvable decision to the unsolvable problems that confront us.

This posture or perspective sets us over against all " intrinsicalist" ethics, against all "given" or " natural" or " objectively valid" laws and maxims, whether of the natural law or the Scriptural law varieties.

The situationist holds that whatever is the most loving thing in the situation is the right and good thing (*Situation Ethics,* Joseph Fletcher, pg. 65, The Westminster Press).

According to Fletcher, we may deviate from the natural, moral or governmental laws if a situation so demands and the guiding principle in those situations is love.

A common objection to Situation Ethics is that it calls for more critical intelligence, more factual information, and more self-starting commitment to righteousness than most people can bring to bear (*Situation Ethics,* Joseph Fletcher, pg. 81).

As possible examples of the moral law versus the new morality, or in Fletcher's terms, Situation Ethics, the admonition "thou shalt not steal" is clear, but what if a starving child requires the mother to steal for the child's survival? What if the "do not kill" suddenly requires termination of life as in the Terri Shivo case? What if adultery is demanded for one's survival in a war camp, for instance?

Does the present world call for a "new morality," a different approach to sort out the complex issues that confront all of modern society? There are theologians, religious thinkers, and modernists who think so.

Admittedly there are situations where the absolute truths of the above-mentioned laws call for added prudent analysis, understanding, and discernment, but to deviate from foundation laws upon which our society is constructed and established is wrong and unnecessary. We live in a society that institutes laws to protect ourselves and others. They are a code of conduct. Whether governmental laws or the Ten Commandments or other religious precepts of conduct, they are instituted to enable humans to live and respect one another. We are guided by one or both of these institutions: the law of the land and spiritual guidelines. Can a "new morality" supersede the old? Can it offer "advanced" insight into the complex issues of our present society? Does it, will it, can it be the solve-all guide to modern society? Will it differ from the Mosaic code we all structure our conduct and behavior by? The Mosaic code will be around until the end of time. Jesus stated the fact that:

> *Do not think that I [Jesus] have come to abolish the Law or the Prophets; I have not come to abolish them but to fulfill them. I tell you the truth, until heaven and earth disappear, not the smallest letter, not the least stroke of a pen; will by any means disappear from the Law until everything is accomplished.*
>
> —Matthew 5:17-18

A new morality? Jesus already did that. He took the Mosaic Law and added teeth to it by the defining habits of the heart. It is more than the act; it is intent of the heart. The old law said, "You shall not commit adultery," but Jesus said "whoever looks on a woman with lust has already committed adultery."

To operate on a predicate of love in all situations is dangerous ground and should be a cautious path. Love is subjective and left to interpretation. Love is not subject to the foundations of a moral code.

CHAPTER 12

CHOOSING GOD

"We are because God is."

—Emanuel Swedenborg

WE CHOOSE GOD because He first chose us. That choosing occurred when He uttered the words, "let us make man in our image." The depth and the breadth of what that means have mystified intelligent beings since creation. The whys of why God would want to make us in His image are both confounding and awe-inspiring, but he had His reasons and we are the benefactors of that act of communion. As our part of His creation, He set us as caretakers of the earth: to subdue it, to explore it, to be stewards of it.

But there is something more spiritual than merely being stewards of the earth. King David pondered the reasons for God and man's relationship in the Psalms with these words:

> I often think of the heavens your hands have made,
> And of the moon and stars you put in place.
> Then I ask, "Why do you care about us humans?
> Why are you concerned for us weaklings?"
> You made us a little lower than you yourself,
> And you have crowned us with glory and honor.

You let us rule everything your hands have made.
And you put all of it under our power—the sheep
And the cattle, and every wild animal, and the birds
In the sky, the fish in the sea, and all ocean creatures.

Our Lord and Ruler, your name is wonderful
Everywhere on earth!

—Psalm 8:3-9 (CEV)

God wants a relationship with His created beings and thus made us to be like Him. We are intelligent, inventive, creative, communicative, and have free will. Yet God is perfect in all His ways. He wants us to be like Him and thus has innately placed a monitor of right and wrong within us—our conscience. Even more importantly, He has placed a longing and knowledge that our lives are not complete in and of ourselves. Without Him we are incomplete. "In all of our hearts lies a longing for a Sacred Romance," says John Eldredge. That completeness is only possible when we are in a relationship with our heavenly Father. As the hymn of the church says, "there is a place of quiet rest near to the heart of God, a place where sin cannot molest…a place of full release and a place where all is joy and peace, near to the heart of God." (text and music by Cleland B. McAfee)

God has continually reached out to His people throughout time. Even when we humans performed the first act of disobedience by ignoring His command to not eat from the tree of the knowledge of good and evil, God pronounced He would put enmity between Satan and man. He did that through the sacrificial act on the cross of Calvary when Jesus died for the sins of mankind. That is Christianity's central theme. God became man to be one of us and to establish His kingdom on this earth.

Obviously, this writing is from the Christian perspective and does not take into account the belief systems of other religions. Traditionally we view God as Creator, an all-powerful, all-knowing, all-sustaining presence in the universe. That is the Judeo-Christian's principle foundation and is the central theme in all of Scripture. God is indeed the creator of all mankind, but monotheism is not recognized as such in many religions or sects.

Defining the term "religion" is a complex and subjective process and one that boggles the mind trying to sort it all out. I hesitate to use the term in the context of this work as the definition causes more confusion than clarity. Yet it is important that we encompass a belief system in the topic of choice for many reasons. First, religion is a powerful motivator. It satisfies man's inward expression to find purpose outside of himself—the searching of things larger and higher than his mind can answer. The unsearchable questions of life and unquenchable thirst for meaning are religion's quest. Second, its rewards and the good that come from it are indeed profound. It has benefits far exceeding its superficiality. People are happier, live longer, and feel better about themselves when involved in the experiences of a religious order. Third, it enables us to make wise choices by directing our priorities toward things higher than ourselves. It instills in us the desire for a greater good—to be peacemakers, doers of right, and stewards of our family, our fellow man, and the earth.

Most of us don't really set out to choose a religion for ourselves. Not that that can't be done, but it generally is not the way we find meaning for ourselves. Most of the religious notions, practice, or levels of devoutness come from our traditions, family, or culture. If born Protestant, Catholic, Muslim, Jewish, or Buddhist, to name only a few, we are likely to continue those traditions and cultures throughout our lives. We are preprogrammed to accept and adopt those influences in our upbringing. Our individual choices don't have much to do with it. The choice, however, to change or continue or even to disband our belief system is ours, and ours alone, to make. There comes a point in our maturity where we individually decide that having a belief system or not, is important to us.

So far we have talked about the positive side of religion. There is a negative side. Under the guise of religion, beliefs mean many things to different cultures, sects, and faiths. Madeleine Albright declares in her book, *The Mighty and the Almighty,* "Religion is perhaps the single largest influence in shaping the human conscience, and yet it is also a source of conflict and hate." Religion doesn't have a good record in the history of the world. Often with the efforts to Christianize or impose religion on others, we brutalize or oppress or kill. Whether under the canopy of radical beliefs of Islam, the Crusades of the Middle Ages, the conflicts in Northern Ireland, the Arab-Israeli conflicts, the brutal spread of Christianity to the Aztecs, or the present Iraqi sectarian conflict, religion has set a bad example in and to the world.

When and if we choose a religion for ourselves, that choice should be one of benefit—benefit for the individual and the community. What is the purpose of believing if not for the good of the humankind and to add meaning to our living? Any purpose other than these would be a bad choice. If a religion controls to the point of extreme fanaticism then it could be detrimental, oppressive, or life threatening to us, the community, and our families.

The Christian teaching of "do unto others as you would have them do to you" rests all the law and the prophets, says Jesus, but this concept is not unique to Western thought. Many religions have similar statements in their creed.

> Hinduism demands that "no man do to another that which would be repugnant to himself." The Torah instructs us, "thou shalt love thy neighbor as myself." Zoroaster observed, "What I hold good for myself, I should for all." Confucius said, "What you do not want done to yourself, do not unto others." Buddha taught us to consider others as ourselves. The Stoics of ancient Greece argued that all men are "equal persons in the great court of liberty." The Christian gospel demands, "Do unto others as you would have done unto you." The Quran warns that a true believer must love for his brother what he loves for himself. Finally, the world's first known legal code had as its announced purpose "to cause justice to prevail and to ensure that the strong do not oppress the weak."
>
> —Madeleine Albright
> *The Mighty and the Almighty,* pg. 290

How then, when we have the same basic creed amongst most all religions, can we distort those teachings to the detriment of society and people of the world?

When we are commanded under Christianity to "Love the Lord thy God with all thy heart, mind and soul" and "love thy neighbor as thyself," how can that be translated into anything but good for society?

When or at what point does one's religion pass from "You shall know the truth and the truth will make you free" to grip or rob one's mind of free choice? God never meant an experience or belief in Him to be oppressive or burdensome. Religion should be a liberator not oppressor. "I am come that you might have life and have it more abundantly," says Jesus. Ask any Christian if he or she is liberated or oppressed and see what the answer will be.

Our involvement in religion, our spiritual walk with God, various aspects of Christianity, or even our indifference toward any of it is central to our understanding of who we are and our place in the world, society, our culture, and God's purpose for our own lives. We can make choices independent of it or can be included in it.

Back to the idea that God continually reaches out to us. If that then is the case, we might ask ourselves the question, to what extent is God involved in the affairs of men?

We might acknowledge that God is sovereign and He reigns over the affairs of humankind, but do we think He is actively involved in the day-to-day details of our own personal lives? Does He care about us? Does He want the best for us?

Many have asked those questions and still ask, "Is God really in control of the minute details of the affairs of the world or even my own life?" And the answer is Yes! Yes! Yes!, but only if we want Him or even let Him. You see, God doesn't force His agenda on any of us; He lets us do as we choose.

I have wondered and pondered, just as any other person has, about why God chooses to be silent when we expect otherwise. The many questions of why He let so and so happen, or why doesn't He intervene in a particular situation or why didn't He prevent the holocausts of the past or even the present from occurring? Why did He let Hitler or Stalin or Idi Amin or Sadaam Hussein or many others have power? Why does He let some suffer and others not? Why are there many poor people compared to the rich? Why the disparity?

In his book, *Ask Him Anything,* Lloyd J. Ogilvie says:

There are three presuppositions, which must guide our answer to all the questions about God's involvement in our…existence. First,

God is supremely in control when he limits his control. Second, he is sensitively in control as he grants us the gift of free will, knowing what we may do with it. Third, he is sublimely in control as he intervenes and brings good out of evil that happens to and around us. (pgs.25,26)

The biblical statement in Romans 8:28 says, "And we know that in all things God works for the good of those who love him, who have been called according to his purpose." This is one of the most comforting and revealing scriptures in the entire Bible.

The often uttered phrase, "it was meant to happen" or "I'll go whenever it is my time" or "she and I were meant for each other," implies that there is a greater force than us who is controlling the events of our lives. We say these things not really knowing why we say them. Maybe we really do think there is a destiny out there for us; that there is something or somebody that is looking out for us and arranging life's circumstances on our behalf. And, if this scenario were true, does it happen for all of us, all of mankind?

King David would say that God knew him as he was even in his mother's womb and that He knows our every motion, thought, response, or action. It is confirmed in the statement, "All things work together for those who love God and are called to according to his purpose." We are all called according to His purpose, but not all of us choose to respond or believe or follow.

Is God actively involved in the affairs of all of our lives? I think the answer falls into two different views: the secular and the spiritual.

Secular Minded

All activities of a so-called secular lifestyle eliminate the possibility of religious, spiritual, or godly influence. This statement is not meant to be an exclusive opinion that participants are not religious or do not believe in God; rather, it implies that secular-minded individuals do not include Divine Providence or spiritual influence in our own choices or by-chance happenings. Sometimes, however, everyday language may imply otherwise.

Secular-minded individuals have no religious or spiritual definitions to explain life or the occurrences that affect them and will go out of their way to avoid direct reference to the one true authority—Almighty God. They are victims or recipients of good or bad fortune (luck) and accept what life deals out. They think they are in control of their own destiny.

Even then, most people think that in the end, regardless of their belief system, everyone goes to heaven, or at least to a place of good. This is odd—to think that we all might spend an eternity with God when we haven't even acknowledged His presence or bothered to get to know Him in this life.

If we have this view of life, the view where God is absent from the circumstances of our life, can we expect Him to be at our beckoning call when we need Him?

Spiritually Minded

When we believe in God and accept His Son, Jesus Christ, as the Savior of our lives and have turned from our sin then we are called the sons of God. We are His chosen people and we are the heirs of the kingdom. If we haven't come to that place then we are not children of God and do not have salvation; we therefore cannot expect God to be involved in the affairs of our lives.

God does want us to be part of His kingdom and wishes all people be saved. It is our choice, however. It is not God who will say who will or won't—it is us.

For God so loved the world that he gave his one and only Son, that whoever believes in him shall not perish but have eternal life. For God did not send his Son into the world to condemn the world, but to save the world through him. Whoever believes in him is not condemned but whoever does not believe stands condemned already because he has not believed in the name of God's one and only Son

—John 3:16-18

Yet, and there is always a "yet" or a "but" where God is concerned, God is omnipotent, omnipresent, and eternal. He not only created the world and all that is in it, but knows intimately the affairs of every person's life and wants everyone to be part of His agenda.

Remember the story of Joseph in chapter two? That introduction was intended to show how God deals with His chosen people under the most diverse of human circumstances. Here is the finish to that story as told in the last fifteen chapters of Genesis where God uses individuals for His purposes.

Many years passed with Joseph going through various phases of trials and fortunes. Those are interesting stories in and of themselves, however, for this part, Pharaoh had dreams that were interpreted only by Joseph. He predicted that Egypt would go through seven years of plenty and seven years of famine. Pharaoh put Joseph in charge of the whole land of Egypt. He was second in command.. During the seven years of plenty, Joseph collected and stored grain. And during the seven-year famine he distributed the food as needed by the people. Other countries were also in famine including his father Jacob and his family.

Having learned there was food and grain in Egypt, Jacob sent his ten sons down to buy food. The sons of Jacob met their brother Joseph but did not recognize him assuming he was dead long ago. However Joseph recognized his ten brothers and questioned them severely as to their father and other siblings. They confessed they had a younger brother named Benjamin. "Go back to Canaan and bring back your younger brother," Joseph commanded. "Meanwhile I will keep one of the others in prison until you return."

The nine brothers returned to Canaan and to their father with the news and with some food to sustain them for a while. Joseph was reluctant to let Benjamin go down to Egypt with the other bothers but finally consented by necessity of life. When Joseph's brothers returned to Egypt, Joseph held a feast on their behalf and with a burst of emotion, revealed himself to his eleven siblings.

"Go back," Joseph said, "to Canaan and bring our father and all that is in his household to Egypt and I will sustain you here in the land of Goshen." So they did. All the family, their possessions, livestock, and servants traveled to the land of Goshen to live while the famine was only two years into the seven-year plague.

Jacob was old and near death, but blessed his sons and requested to be buried in his homeland. So Jacob died and was embalmed according to the process of Egyptian tradition.

Now that Jacob was dead, the brothers were afraid that Joseph might take vengeance on them for the wrong they had done to him.

This is one of the finest passages in all of Scripture and the point of this brief story.

> When Joseph's brothers saw that their father was dead, they said, "What if Joseph holds a grudge against us and pays us back for all the wrongs we did to him?" So they sent word to Joseph, saying, "your father left these instructions before he died: 'this is what you are to say to Joseph: I ask you to forgive your brothers the sins and the wrongs they committed in treating you so badly.'" When their message came to him, Joseph wept. His brothers then came and threw themselves down before him. "We are your slaves," they said. But Joseph said to them, "Don't be afraid. Am I in the place of God? You intended to harm me, but God intended it for good to accomplish what is now being done, the saving of many lives. So then, don't be afraid, I will provide for you and your children." And he reassured them and spoke kindly to them.
>
> —Genesis 50:15-21

In short, God uses people for His purposes. Whether they are children of God or not, He makes all things work together for His ultimate purpose. He can use the derelict, the corporate executive, the priest, the postal worker, the churchgoer, and any number of other people to work for His good. He is the master networker. What an awesome God we serve.

The Two of Us: The Spiritual and the Physical

We are all two distinct yet interwoven individuals: physical and spiritual. Neither of these is exclusive of the other as both are intimately involved in our being. But we spend more time developing or nurturing the physical rather than the spiritual part of our needs—especially the mystic spiritual experience. We are mostly physically driven as we think about the body's necessities like food, sleep, appearance, athleticism; we are spiritual in our thinking, creativity, artistic development, emotions, cognitive development, self-actualization, comfort, success, prayer, and religious fulfillment.

Spiritual means an intimate connection with God, where, with all our actions, thoughts, decisions, and choices, we are conscious of God's input in our lives and call upon Him constantly and place our complete trust and security in Him. Does life favor us because of that? Or, does God favor us over the secular individual? Are our lives better, do we get the good of life? I would have to say an astounding yes to that, and then say no. The spiritual person has insight, wisdom, and a view of life the secular person does not have. "Eye has not seen, nor ear heard, nor has it entered into the heart of man the things the Lord has prepared for those who love Him" (1 Corinthians 2:9). As Jesus said, "I am come that you might have life and have it more abundantly." Does God guide us if we seek Him? And bless us if we follow His commandments and do what He wants us to do? Yes! Are we immune to sickness, disease, death, financial problems, marital, friend or family problems, suffering, or persecution? No! But the promise of Romans 8:28 is: "For we know that God causes all things to work together for the good of those who love God and are called according to His purpose." As Christians, we should take great comfort in that verse for it says so many things about our purpose, our life, our choosing. If we break it down, it might be explained as follows:

- For we know…we have great confidence in, our faith is grounded in the hope and assurance that "God is our refuge and strength, a very present hope in trouble," and in life.
- God causes…God is the omnipotent omnipresent overseer of the events of our life. He makes things happen on our behalf and for His purposes. This life is not just a happenstance for us, but a real cause.
- Everything…not just a few things or the things we ask for, but every event, happening, situation, trouble, good, etc., is under God's ruling hand.
- To work together…all of life and the compilation of events work together. Not separately, but together. Not only the events of

our life, but the events of our collective lives and the events of the world.

- For the good…God causes everything to work together for the good, not the bad. We might not think that the events of our life are going well, or because we have misfortune or illness or death or whatever else, but we can be assured according to this promise, that God is causing all things to work together for the good.

- To those who love God and are called according to His purpose: This is an exclusive club. It's only for those who love God and have chosen to follow in the footsteps of Jesus Christ and keep His commandments. It's for Christians only and not the secular minded. Is God discriminating? No, not at all. He wishes all would become part of His family and His purpose. What is God's purpose? What is His agenda? What are His purposes for us? Solomon says that our whole duty is to fear God and keep His commandments.

As John Eldredge says in his book *The Sacred Romance*, "Every human being is of great significance to God, but those whom God has drawn to believe in him are center stage in a drama of cosmic proportions."

What comfort that statement is; it gives assurance that we are under the umbrella of God's guidance. This is Divine Providence at work.

Back to the question, does God favor us as believers? Of course He does. He is our vision. First Corinthians 2:10-16 (CEV) states:

God's spirit has shown you everything. His Spirit finds out everything, even what is deep in the mind of God. You are the only one who knows what is in your own mind, and God's Spirit is the only one who knows what is in God's mind. But God has given us his Spirit. That's why we don't think the same way that the people of this world think. That's the blessings that God has given us.

Every word we speak was taught to us by God's Spirit, not by human wisdom. And this same Spirit helps us teach spiritual things to spiritual people. That's why only someone who has God's Spirit can understand spirit blessings. Any one who doesn't have God's Spirit thinks these blessings are foolish. People who are guided by the spirit can make all kinds of judgments, but they cannot be judged by others.

The Scriptures ask, "Has anyone ever known the thoughts of the Lord or given him advice?"
But we understand what Christ is thinking.

What about the life of the unbeliever, the agnostic, the atheist? What about the events of their lives? Does God not guide them at all? Is there no outside influence to their life? Are they left to their own devices and plans? Is there no ultimate purpose to life? Is there no direction?

God can and does use situations, circumstances, and people for His purposes. He can use the Christian, the unbeliever, the politician, world affairs, and any number of other devices for His cause. Again, He is the master networker.

The verse of Romans 8:28 is quite clear. It is for those who love God. He of course welcomes anyone and encourages everyone to become the sons of God. Any who wish to believe in Him and accept Jesus Christ as the one who died on the cross for the sins of mankind and rose again so that we might have life, are under God's guiding hand.

It is a clear choice and one of obvious power—the power to accept God's promises or not.

Walking in Faith

Faith has a significant place in the matter of choice. Faith and belief in God is an act of will and a deliberate choice. Faith, like electricity, radio waves, gravity, magnetism, and even love, is an unseen reality, and act of the will is choosing to believe because the evidence and the result is there. How do we express love? How do we know we love our spouses, friends, parents, animals? That unseen reality is real and there are mountains of evidence that express that undefined reality. Faith is the fact that God is real—as real as the tree in my backyard.

We criticize faith as a non-reality—something that cannot be proven by evidence and scientific scrutiny. But every day we cast our very lives on faith. We utilize the unknown for our benefit. If you don't think that is true, think about these: we eat in restaurants, visit doctors, and accept medicine without knowledge of what we are taking, eating, or drinking. We travel in automobiles where the risk is surprisingly high, use electricity or any other electronic device without understanding, have faith in our broker, insurance agent, and politicians and trust a thousand other things that we know nothing about.

But is this different than believing in God? And if so, how so?

> Now faith is being sure of what we hope for and certain of what we do not see…And without faith it is impossible to please God, because anyone who comes to him must believe that he exists and that he rewards those who earnestly seek him.
> —Hebrews 11:1,6

"Draw nigh to God and he will draw nigh to you" says the apostle James. I wish it weren't that way. There are so many that will not or have not the desire to draw close to God. It would seem that God doesn't go out of His way to reveal Himself and sometimes He is purposefully silent. Yet He is everywhere and in all things.

This scripture says that you can't come to the Father unless the spirit draws you. I know God reaches out. I know there is evidence of the presence of God. I know God is everywhere. God knows who is interested and who isn't. God will reveal Himself to those who are and for those who aren't, the evidence is abundant.

Choosing to see, choosing to hear is revealing. Choosing to see God is an eye and ear opener. I see because I choose to see. The enabler is faith. "Once I was blind but now I see."

God, I See You

God, there are those who say You don't exist, but Lord, I keep seeing You.

God, there are many who ignore You, who don't think of You, who don't acknowledge You; But Lord, everywhere I see You.

God, there are those who need to see but somehow choose otherwise.

Lord, I see You and hear You in music, in the sounds of nature. If I look at the heavens, You are there. I hear You and feel You when the wind blows, when it rains, when it's hot.

I see You in the colors of the fall, in the flowers of spring, in the birth of a child, in the intricacy of the human form, in the simplicity of water.

I see You in the mighty power of a hurricane, in the gentle flight of a bird that lands softly on a twig, or in the sweetness of sugarcane.

I see You in the peeling of an orange, in the pockets of sweet juices, of the taste of sweet tartness.

I see You in others: transformed lives, lives full of joy and purpose, of goodness, of peace.

I see You in me, in the transformation of my thinking, in the assurance of salvation, in the mysteries of faith, in the confidence that You are my Lord and my God.

God, I don't know why You allow me to see, but thank You!

We can make no greater choice in this life than accepting God's call to join Him in His kingdom. The benefits, the peace that surpasses all understanding, the assurance of salvation and the promise that we will live forever as heirs of the kingdom is surely an offer we can't refuse. God chooses us, let us choose Him.

CHAPTER 13

WHAT ABOUT LUCK?

IF WE LOOK at the events that happen to us, we might wonder about the sources of those happenings. Life certainly dishes out a variety of events that happen to everyone. Supposedly these many things are outside of our grasp and just part of the circumstances of life.

Life does consist of random events, chance happenings or what we call luck, good and bad (accidents, victims of crime, near misses, winnings of chance, and a host of other things beyond our control), Divine Providence, and our own choices. And just to make life more interesting, let's throw in fate, destiny, serendipity, and even coincidence just to add confusion. But isn't there another category that should fit? Aren't the things that happen to us just plain life? That is, life filled with the good, the bad, and the ugly—sickness, accidents, laughter, enjoyment, family, friends, people we love and those that love us, and on and on. How do we sort out these things?

Leonard Mlodinow, in his book *The Drunkard's Walk,* would say "the outline of our lives, like the candle's flame, is continuously coaxed in new directions by a variety of random events that, along with our responses to them, determine our fate."(pg.4). These events are described as randomness and how it rules our lives, according to Mlodinow.

Many of us conduct our lives by luck, chance, superstition, astrology, or a lackadaisical attitude of whatever happens, happens—a happenstance philosophy.

Take a typical astrological forecast for instance. We are encouraged to go through our day according to the words on a printed page. Since my birth date dictates that I am a Leo, does that presuppose the events of my day or even my destiny? Do my fellow Leos in starving Africa have the same uplifting promise that I generally get by the astrological forecast? Who is the audience relating to the particular date or time? Is it applicable to everyone, like the affluent person, the poor, the starving, and the invalid, or is it just for a select few?

Astrology has its basis in astronomy where the ancients named twelve constellations applicable to the happenings on earth. Since then, many have taken seriously these signs and symbols that are still applicable to our everyday living; and many people (celebrities, historical figures, and everyday folk) are labeled with these Zodiac signs signifying who we are. There is the perception of a thing and then the reality of a thing. The perception is that by some mystic pronouncement from the stars we gain favor by being born under a particular zodiac sign. The reality of life is that we can let those perceptions take hold of our lives or we can take hold of our life and our choices. As for the daily astrograph, my newspaper says this is for entertainment only. That surely is the reality of astrology's purpose.

Is luck and chance happenings the same thing? We might view chance happenings as those occurrences which are out of our and everything else's control, but view luck as an unexpected or hopeful blessing which singles us out as an object of favor.

We all played "Lots" as kids. We called it drawing straws. The person drawing the shortest stick, match, or straw got chosen to be the odd person out or the chosen one of a game. For sure it is a game of pure luck and was an unbiased way of selection. Casting lots was also a method of selection in biblical times with approximately seventy references in the Old Testament and seven in the New.

Consider these two instances of the practices of casting lots:

In the book of Jonah in the first chapter, we read that "the word of the Lord came to Jonah son of Amittai: 'go to the great city of Nineveh and preach against it, because of its wickedness has come up before me.'" But Jonah did not want to preach to the Ninevites and ran away by boarding a ship for Tarshish. A violet storm came up and threatened to break the ship apart. Jonah had gone below decks and fell into a deep sleep. The captain, fearing total destruction, went to Jonah and said, "How can you sleep? Get up and call on your god! Maybe he will take notice of us, and we will not perish."

Then the sailors said to each other, "Come let us cast lots to find out who is responsible for this calamity." They did and the lot fell to Jonah. In this story, lots were more than luck, it was an identifier of a fault or person of faults. It was a recognized process of selection that had mystic powers. The lot fell to Jonah. How? By luck? By Divine Providence? Could the lot have fallen to another?

The short of the story is that Jonah requested he be thrown overboard to save the men and the ship. That they did. The storm subsided.

And another example:

After Judas turned Jesus in to the officials, he hung himself leaving eleven of the original twelve apostles. To complete the apostolic vacancy, the remaining disciples sought to replace him. With the eleven gathered in an upstairs room and with fervent prayer, they sought God's guidance for the person:

> So they proposed two men: Joseph called Barsabbas (also known as Justus) and Matthias. Then they prayed, "Lord, you know everyone's heart. Show us which of these two you have chosen to take over this apostolic ministry, which Judas left to go where he belongs. Then they cast lots, and the lot fell to Matthias; so he was added to the eleven apostles.
>
> —Acts 1:23-26

Can we say that God's hand was involved in these two incidences? Isn't it odd that games of chance were used in selecting the right person in each situation? Can lots then be used to determine choices in our lives? They could if we choose to make choices by that process, but I think the game of drawing straws falls mostly toward random chance rather than God's Providence.

Luck

Let's explore luck. Luck is those fortunes and misfortunes that come our way that are none of our doing.

The word luck is used so much in conversation that one would think it a real thing: a thing that has purpose, that singles out people to bless, that has the best intentions for people, that is a force to reckon with, that is looked upon with respect and sacredness, that is out there drifting around searching for a person to cast a lucky spell upon.

Take for instance the phrase taken from a Dear Abby column, which concludes, " I wish her the best of luck." Luck then, in this instance might seem to indicate there are levels of luck—bad, not-so-bad, good, better, and the best. And whatever lucky force there is out in the universe, the request indicated that luck would look upon her with favor, and, not only with favor, but the best of favor.

I don't like the word luck, but we all use it to express in a concise manner what we mean when life affects us by chance happenings. Often there is not another word out there to replace it. And, it is a matter of convenience and acceptance. It is a product of everyday conversation. What could we say instead? I wish her the best of good fortune? Or, I hope she does well. Or may the force be with her, or bless her lucky stars. Or God speed, or any number of other pronouncements we could speak to wish her well. And luck usually expresses the positive things that occur. The phrase, "they were lucky," expresses good luck and not bad. Some might say, "if I didn't have bad luck, I wouldn't have any luck at all."

But luck can be defined by saying those occurrences that come our way are none of our doing. All of us have those happenings in every day of our living. Some are good and some not so good. But that really does not encompass all of life.

Luck does seem to have two definitions: one being that people use it to express genuine concern for others. For instance, "Good luck with your doctor's appointment next week." Another is the use of luck to express the randomness of events. "I was unlucky at bingo last night."

Do accidents fall into the luck category—good or bad results? Some are preventable for sure, but for the most part, accidents are none of our doing. We are in the wrong place at the wrong time or in the right place at the wrong time.

Bad Luck

The by-chance happenings might be that I decide to cut grass and a stone flies up from the mower and hits me in the head and puts me in the hospital or worse—takes my life. Or I may decide to read a book and that book changes my life. Or I decide to go to college but I come down with a life-threatening disease, or there is a freak accident while riding a bicycle and I am paralyzed for the rest of my life. Are all these because of bad luck or by-chance happenings? Were they preventable? Sometimes. We never ask for or seek bad luck. That would be ridiculous, but we put ourselves in harm's way often, which is a choice. We can have a lifestyle that keeps us out of harm's way as much as possible and that is a choice.

Good Luck

If you listen to television news enough you will notice the language that permeates broadcast journalism. "There was a fire overnight at so and so residence and the Jones family was lucky to get out alive." Or, "Mr. Smith had the lucky lottery number and won one million dollars." Or, "if we are lucky enough, the clear skies will remain with us for several more days."

Or we might even say, "I had an accident and rolled the car three times and walked away without a scratch…I was lucky." Or "I played the lottery and won X amount of money," "the storm did not hit us," "we were lucky," or "if my luck holds out then…"

Take the game show program called *Deal or No Deal* where contestants are offered a million dollars by selecting silver briefcases that have various sums of money in the total of 26 cases ranging from one cent to a million dollars. The choice is to select a case that has the million dollars in it. Then during the process reduce the choices down to a level where the participant feels comfortable with their current winnings or risks further gains or losses. The choices are many: to risk, be satisfied, to select random numbers, or quit the game. It is still the whims of chance. The game is pure chance, and not luck.

Life can be like that: gambling, living on the edge, taking chances, not preparing, and having the attitude, "whatever will be will be."

We would be led to believe that our lives are a mere coincidence and subject to the whims of chance.

What a fearful way to live. I would hate to think my life is run on the whims of chance.

Whether or not we choose to believe in luck or fortune or horoscopes as guides to our living, life can still slant to our favor if we choose.

As the Amish proverb says, "the harder I work the luckier I am." Or as Randy Pausch says in his book *The Last Lecture*, "luck is what happens when preparation meets opportunity." This is one of Randy's favorite quotes from the Roman philosopher Seneca. That philosophy has been the work ethic of many notables: Tiger Woods, Edison, the Wright Brothers, George Washington Carver, the Olympic athletes, and many of us.

Who's to say if any of life's situations or circumstances is luck, fate, destiny, or providence? I certainly would not rule out God's hand in any of life's situations.

Consider the story of Alexander Fleming: Fleming found penicillin purely by accident, but he had the knowledge to realize his discovery. While working on experiments relating to staphylococci, he left culture dishes unclean in his laboratory. After returning from a long vacation, Fleming noticed many of his culture dishes were contaminated with a fungus and preceded to put them in disinfectant solution. Meanwhile, a visitor wanted to know what he was working on. He retrieved some fungus samples not yet dipped in the cleaning solution. He discovered a zone around the fungus where the bacteria had not grown. Hence the discovery of a substance he named Penicillin.

Had Fleming not been well-trained in medicine and more than an active interest in experimentation, he would not have discovered a substance that would eventually save millions of lives. Hard work, dedication, and education were key ingredients in his story, or even our own stories. Yet, one important ingredient interplayed here—was it luck, a chance happening, or Divine Providence? You decide.

How do we evaluate all these scenarios of life? We often cannot control what happens to us but can control our reactions to it. We control our attitudes about it.

Mostly up to this point we have considered luck from the secular perspective. What about from the Christian viewpoint?

We have already discussed the pros and cons of the secular life versus the spiritual life where we depend on God for our purpose, our mission in life, our daily bread.

The Christian should view luck entirely differently. It should not even be in their vocabulary, as nothing happens to the Christian without God's permission. We don't depend on luck, or the stars, or happenstance, or the hit and miss theory of life, but upon God.

In Jesus' Sermon on the Mount He says:

Therefore I tell you, do not worry about your life, what you will eat or drink; or about your body, what you will wear. Is not life more important than food, and the body more important than clothes? Look at the birds of the air; they do not sow or reap or store away in barns, and yet your heavenly Father feeds them. Are you not more valuable than they? Who of you by worrying can add a single hour to his life?

And why do you worry about clothes? See how the lilies of the field grow. They do not labor or spin. Yet I tell you that not even Solomon in all his splendor was dressed like one of these. If that is how God clothes the grass of the field, which is here today and tomorrow is thrown into the fire, will he not much more clothe you, O you of little faith?

So do not worry, saying 'What shall we eat?' or 'What shall we drink?' or 'What shall we wear?' For the pagans run after all these things, and your heavenly Father knows that you need them. But seek first his kingdom and his righteousness, and all these things will be given to you as well. Therefore do not worry about tomorrow, for tomorrow will worry about itself. Each day has enough trouble of its own.

—Matthew 6:25-34

If then, as this scripture says, God takes care of His own, how does luck enter into life? It doesn't. The godly person places his faith in one that has control of all of life: the accidents, the actions of people, the future, and the reasons of what happens to us. The secular minded can only identify the causes of life as luck or chance or…

Life's randomness is secular; God's divine order is spiritual and purposeful. We can choose astrology, luck, the whims of life, or we can choose to recognize that God is the pilot of our lives.

CHAPTER 14

LIBERTY, FREEDOM, AND CHOICE

We hold these truths to be self-evident, that all men are created equal, that they are endowed by their Creator with certain unalienable Rights, that among these are Life, Liberty and the pursuit of Happiness.

—Declaration of Independence

THE DEMOCRACY WE enjoy as Americans is a unique political structure contrasted to all other governments in the world. The framing of our Declaration of Independence from England, the derivation of the constitution, the Bill of Rights, and the American ideal is "our common creed." Our democracy was formed under the premise that the established government shall be under the consent of the governed. That we will establish ourselves with certain unalienable rights and frame those rights in a document labeled the Bill of Rights. No one can take these away from us; no one can separate us from the bond that makes us free. It dictates our past and secures and ensures our future.

That central ideal is our unique American heritage. While our govennmental structure is exclusively an American thought, the fact that all men are created equal and are endowed by our Creator with certain rights should not for us alone, it is for all peoples.

We must never forget that the freedoms we possess as Americans came from the sacrifices of others and other generations. Often they came at a price through blood, sweat, and tears, and on occasion the ultimate sacrifice of giving one's life for our freedom and liberty. While we may think our choices are ours only, we must remember that someone (our parents, caregivers, the government, ancestors, veterans), provided the opportunity or the circumstances to allow us to make choices. We have inherited this life and are now caretakers of it. The choices we make, as the earth's present generation, will not only affect our own families and our own culture, but the following generations as well. The legacy we leave as this generation passes from us, good or bad, for the betterment of man or not, for the good of the earth or not, should instill an awesome sense of responsibility on us.

And, we can't forget those who have helped us along the way—those who supported us, nurtured us, mentored us, inspired us, and put a vision in our heads. They may have been friends, spouses, parents, teachers, strangers, or angels unaware, but whoever they are, we did not arrive where we are by ourselves. Never does one succeed by oneself. The phrase "he is a self-made man" is really never true. The climb to whatever status we desire to achieve or have achieved did not occur by our own power. We may think that that's true. But a host of people helped paved our way to the top—whether we used them or abused them.

It is not our choice to be free or have freedom. That is something that was given, a gift handed to us. There was a time when freedom was the American choice—a choice to acquire, to covet, to die for. We have freedom in this country whether we want it or not. We can enjoy the blessings of freedom whether or not we buy into the democratic philosophy or not. We can enjoy the blessings of God whether or not we believe in Him. That is another freedom. It is, however, our choice to maintain our American freedom.

We can do that in several ways: we can appreciate, be grateful for, and honor those who made it possible to enjoy this freedom. We can study, read, and educate ourselves in the formation of this unique government. We can participate in its survival, in the perpetuation of its purposes, in the correction of its wrongs and in the prayerful support of its operation.

With liberty and freedom come responsibility, and with responsibility, obedience. Liberty and freedom aren't just buzz words in the political arena. They are words that penetrate our whole existence. Whether that freedom comes from government, or marriage, or our contract with our employer, or our commitment to God, we are obligated, bound, and committed to its end.

As said before, our choices have consequences, affecting us and those around us. What right do we have to make a choice and not be obedient to it?

CHAPTER 15

TOOLS FOR MAKING
WISE CHOICES

T HERE ARE WAYS we can prep ourselves to make good choices by recognizing the power of choice and the awesome responsibility that comes with that recognition.

A friend of mine once said that everyone should major in mathematics as it is training for a logical mind, and then read a hundred of the best books. I have my own version of developing tools for wise choices.

- Be prepared: plan ahead
- Read
- Do: be a doer, an activist, a proactive initiator, accomplish things
- Seek: wisdom, God's will, understanding, knowledge
- Knock: knock at the doors of opportunity
- Ask: ask questions
- Pray: tap into the power of prayer
- Never give up
- Adjust your attitude. Positive attitudes breed positives.

Time

Time is the coin of your life. It is the only coin you have, and only you can determine how it will be spent. Be careful lest you let other people spend it for you.

—Carl Sandburg

Every human on the planet has something in common—time. If we live the average life span of the present 78.2 years, we each have the same amount of hours, days, weeks, and years. How we choose to spend that allotted time is entirely up to us. We are our master personal time-keeper.

As far as choice and time is concerned, we can kill it, waste it, squander it, wish it away, or utilize it to its greatest potential. The average American spends approximately three-fourths of life on the necessities of living: eating, sleeping, working, commuting, traveling, and securing health and happiness. That leaves precious little time for what we might call the pleasures of life. Not that all the above can't be elements of quality of life, but so-called leisure time, which we all covet, is fading from the basic tenets of living.

The proper utilization of time is an important tool in aiding our choices. There have been volumes written on time management, all of it intended to encourage us to use time to the fullest extent, to utilize it to enhance our quality of life and make us more efficient. Some of us need time organization, some don't care, and some under-utilize it.

It is important to recognize that time is a tool for our benefit. How we spend our time coin is our choice.

Conscience

So I strive always to keep my conscience clear before God and man.
—Acts: 24:16

The conscience has a two-fold purpose: it is a moral guide and a tempering spirit.

God has instilled a voice, a barometer if you will, in each of us to speak of the impending wrongs that we might do. The conscience will speak to us if we choose to listen to it. That doesn't mean we can't wear it down until such time the line between right and wrong is no longer there. It is like cogs on a gear; use it and abuse it long enough and the cogs get worn to the point of being useless. Ignore your inner voice and it will no longer speak to you.

Is conscience a tool in the power of choice? By all means. What better guide to choosing than our own internal voice that directs our thoughts to the rights and from the wrongs.

Attitude

Our attitude to life, toward the circumstances, events, and happenings that affect us will determine our reaction to it. Life will deal out to us all sorts of things: sorrow, pain and suffering, misfortune, death, happiness, joy and good times. It is our reaction to them that will help us through the difficult times and appreciate the good times in all these events that we live through.

We may not have control of life's inevitable handouts, but whatever situation we find ourselves in, our attitude is our choice.

Chuck Swindol has written one of the most pointed statements on attitude ever written:

> The longer I live, the more I realize the impact of attitude on life. Attitude, to me, is more important than education, than money, than what other people think or say or do. It is more important than appearance, giftedness, or skill. It will make or break a company...a church...a home. The remarkable thing is we have a choice every day regarding the attitude we embrace for that day. We cannot change our past...we cannot change the fact that people act in certain ways. We cannot change the inevitable. The only thing we can do is play on the one string we have, and that is our attitude...I am convinced that life is 10% what happens to me and 90% how I react to it. And so it is with you...we are in charge of our attitudes.

In James W. Moore's book, *Attitude Is Your Paintbrush*, he describes that attitude colors every situation. He uses the illustration from Dr. Viktor Frankl's book *Man's Search for Meaning*. In it Dr. Frankl, while in a concentration camp in Germany, observed, "we who lived in concentration camps can remember the ones who walked through the huts comforting others...giving away their last piece of bread. They may have been few in number but they offer sufficient proof that everything can be taken from us but one thing: the last of the human freedoms—to choose one's own attitude in any given set of circumstances…to choose one's own way."

Attitude is far reaching. It reaches into every aspect of our existence. It can make us or break us. It can determine our happiness or misery. It can add to our quality of life or leave us depressed. It can make life worth living or leave us only existing. It can make your job worth going to or just a job, it can make your marriage or break it, it can brand you an optimist or a pessimist. It can prolong your life or shorten it. It can make you sick or healthy.

There have been many notable stories of survival; of people who have been placed in life-or-death situations. The overall trait of survival is one's attitude, whether it is war, an accident, being lost, abandoned, or a victim of crime.

Referring back to *Attitude Is Your Paintbrush*, Moore expresses Christian attitudes of gratitude, compassion, confidence, determination, humility, perseverance, open-mindedness, joy, faith, trust, commitment, ownership, and hope as chapter headings. While this book is aimed toward the Christian audience, these expressions of our personality and integrity can follow into the secular arena. An attitude of commitment is our Christian responsibility that follows us in our marriage, our jobs, and every aspect of our daily lives.

Read

"An illiterate crowd is easiest to rule."

—Alberto Manguel

The American writer Frederick Douglass, who was born into slavery and became one of the most eloquent abolitionists of his day as well as founder of several political journals, recalled in his autobiography:

> The frequent hearing of my mistress reading the Bible—for she often read aloud when her husband was absent-- soon awakened my curiosity in respect to this mystery of reading, and roused in me the desire to learn. Having no fear of my kind mistress before my eyes, I frankly asked her to teach me to read; and, without hesitation, the dear woman

began the task, and very soon by her kind assistance, I had mastered the alphabet and could spell words of three or four letters.

—Frederick Douglass
My Bondage and My Freedom (pg 117)

Douglass goes on to say that he was resolute in his desire to read and later in life became a great orator and writer.

Reading cannot be stressed enough. Reading opens one's mind and creates thinking, creativity, and imagination. Reading is to the mind as exercise to the body. Reading develops, creates, opens, thinks, understands, and develops creativity. Reading provides so many examples of people and situations where wisdom, understanding, and wise choices will provide inspiration for us. Those sources are numerous: the Bible, biographies, inspirational writings, the classics, novels, and history.

Most all of the great leaders and intellectuals of the past were voracious readers.

History

History teaches everything, even the future.
—Alphonse de Lamartine

If we don't know where we've been, how can we know where we are going? And if we know where we have been, we can alter the future for the better and not repeat the mistakes of the past. That is true whether it be for a nation, a company, a church, a family, and our own individual lives. History provides numerous examples of the choices of the decisions of the moment. It's easy to see in hindsight what the right and wrong of the decisions might have been. We don't have the luxury of knowing the outcome of events; all we can muster are the proper ingredients of a decision and make it. History can give us that insight. Sure, times change. Culture changes, but humans always act the same whether in Socrates' day or ours. The ingredients for a better society are love, joy, peace, patience, gentleness, goodness, faith, meekness, and self-control. And the ingredients for a world in turmoil are hate, envy, greed, selfism, covertness, power, oppression, pride, and indifference. It is within each of us to make the choice of either grouping.

History also helps us appreciate the sacrifices of the ones who came before us. And it should help us appreciate the freedom we presently enjoy through those sacrifices.

Travel and Experience

Reflecting on the events surrounding our recent vacation where we spent a week's time out in the world among family and strangers, observing the goings on of life outside my small view of the world, I came back from those experiences reflecting, wondering, and questioning the points of what we do…what we humans do that is. And I see and observe a world different from the world presented by the confines of our minute experiences.

How or what does this have to do with choice? Much, I think.

First, one has to experience or expose him/herself to the world: to the experiences, the conditions, the ways of different cultures, languages, the way people think, and to learn. We get a broader scope of the world by experiencing it, and we appreciate life through those experiences. We recognize the disparity and contrasting lifestyles between how the affluent live and how the influent struggle with living.

One of the most shocking examples of culture disparities was when my wife and I went on a Caribbean cruise and one of the stops was Venezuela. The juxtaposition between the luxuriousness of the cruise ship and the poverty of the outskirts of Caracas was both appalling and sobering. I could have easily forgotten the experience of that event, but fifteen years later, it still haunts my memory. I still see the poverty, the thousands of tin roof shacks dotting the hilly landscape on the way to the city.

We make choices based on our experiences. Seeing cultures different from ours will either incite an appreciation of our own blessings or impassion us to change the plight of the poor, the unfortunate, and the oppressed. And further, having a broad view of the world arms us with the ingredients for our own good choices.

Ask, Seek, Knock

Ask and it will be given to you; seek and you will find; knock and the door will be opened to you. For every one who asks receives; and who seeks finds; and to the one who knocks, the door will be opened.

—Matthew 7:7-8

The world is open to the one who seeks, knocks, and asks. It has to do with proactive enthusiasm, quenching the insatiable appetite for knowledge, answers, and fulfillment. It is our Christian duty. God desires our best and is satisfied with nothing less.

Ask

"Ask not what your country can do for you but what you can do for your country."

—John F. Kennedy

Most of our childhood consists of asking. That is how we learn. When we become adults our asking diminishes because we are too embarrassed to question or find out the answers to our questions of life. However, we are apt to ask when we pray—Lord give me this, provide me with the things I need, tell me what to do, give me direction, bless me.

Our asking becomes what will the Lord or my country, or my employer, or my family do for me.

The asking should be a positive incentive and in Scripture asking is quite clear. "Ask anything in my name and I will do it," says Jesus. And, "If you believe, you will receive whatever you ask for in prayer."

Seek

Seek the purpose for your life.

"All men should strive to learn before they die what they are running from and to, and why."

—James Thurber

I have spent a good portion of my life trying to figure out God's will, often to the point of frustration. I'm one of those who find it difficult to make a choice unless I have a clear go or stay or wait. I looked forward with great anxiety, but now look back at my life and see God's guidance. I have learned that the formula for finding God's will is actually quite simple for me and anyone. Actually, it is so simple that we stumble over it, or refuse to participate in it, or want something more difficult. Or perhaps we want the direct revelation from God Himself.

Since most everything in our lives, like the things we do and strive for, are often difficult, we assume finding out God's providence for us must be difficult too. Not so. It has been said that ninety percent of what God wants from us is already revealed in Scripture. For some quick examples, take Proverbs 3:5-6—"Trust in the Lord with all your heart and lean not on your own understanding; in all your ways acknowledge him and he will direct your paths." Or Matthew 6:33, "But seek first his kingdom and his righteousness and all these things will be given to you as well." They are the foundation stones of trust and submission. Those are the keys to knowing. The specifics of what our choices are may not be clear at the moment, but just do. Take God by the hand and just do. Seek that education, that job, that companion, that desire, that talent, that ambition. Some doors will close, some will open, some mistakes will be made, some time might be wasted (we think), but when life's experiences are put together in a package we call our life, we are well equipped to be God's instrument.

Knock

What is the act of knocking? Isn't it persistence, perseverance, practice, repetition, desire, the wanting, and the never-give-up attitude?

We all think of knocking as an act of gaining entry whether it is a house, business, a job, or acknowledgment. God also knocks to get our attention. One of the most famous of pictures is Christ knocking at the door of our hearts. There are actually two famous paintings: *The Light of the World* by William Holman Hunt and *Christ at Heart's Door* by Warner Sallman. Both show Jesus standing outside a door symbolizing knocking at our heart's door. "Behold I stand at the door and knock. If anyone hears my voice and opens the door, I will come in and eat with him, and he with me" (Revelation 3:20).

Knock on the door of opportunity, or rather, *open* the door of opportunity. Opportunity comes in many forms. We want them to come as that perfect job, the vacation we always wanted, those unexpected gifts, or an inheritance from a rich uncle, but often they come as trials, hard work, suffering, patience, and persistence. Sometimes they come serendipitously.

Wisdom, Understanding, and Knowledge

The trio of words (wisdom, understanding, and knowledge), often create a mystique in our minds. We might identify them as perhaps a middle-eastern philosophy or religion that is designated for a few wise prophets or mystery men. We hardly equate them as something we should covet and desire with the whole efforts of our hearts and minds. But that is exactly what Scripture suggests we should do. So we might ask ourselves the question: What is the source of all wisdom, knowledge, and understanding? And what does it matter to me? This passage from the book of Proverbs reveals the answer:

> *My son,* (says Solomon), *if you accept my words and store up my commands within you, turning your ear to wisdom and applying your heart to understanding, and if you call out for insight and cry aloud for understanding, and if You look for it as for silver and search for it as for hidden treasure, then you will understand the fear of the Lord and find the knowledge of God. For the Lord gives wisdom, and from his mouth comes knowledge and understanding.*
> —Proverbs 2:1-6

This scripture implies that there cannot be an ultimate grasp of knowledge, understanding, and wisdom until we have a reverential trust and respect for God as the creator of the universe and all that is in it. Wisdom's foundation is the fear, respect, and reverence for God.

We can be intelligent, smart, have street savvy, have great knowledge, common sense, and a worldly wisdom, but until we come to the place of realizing what is really important in this life…that is, how to live and how to live with others, understand the foundation of real knowledge and understanding through a relationship with God through Jesus Christ, then the knowledge, understanding, and wisdom we have of the world is superficial and incomplete.

"The Scriptures have been expressly formed to be apparent to those who are taught by the Holy Spirit Himself while a closed book to cold reason and precise logic" (pg. 30, *The Holy Spirit*, John F. Walvoord, Dunham Publishing Co., Grand Rapids, MI).

God has given the mystery of the kingdom to those who have chosen to listen and obey the calling of God's message. Paul, in the following passage from 1 Corinthians, has described that special wisdom that only comes from a listening heart:

> We do, however, speak a message of wisdom among the mature, but not the wisdom of this age or of the rulers of this age, who are coming to nothing. No, we speak of God's secret wisdom, a wisdom that has been hidden and that God destined for our glory before time began. None of the rulers of this age understood it, for if they had, they would not have crucified the Lord of glory. However, as it is written, "No eye has seen, no ear has heard, no mind has conceived what God has prepared for those who love him," but God has revealed it to us by his Spirit. The Spirit searches all things, ever the deep things of God. For who among men knows the thoughts of a man except the man's spirit with in him? In the same way no one knows the thoughts of God except the Spirit of God. We have not received the spirit of the world but the Spirit who is from God, that we may understand what God has freely given us.
>
> This is what we speak, not in words thought us by human wisdom but in works taught by the Spirit expressing spiritual truths in spiritual words.
>
> The man without the Spirit does not accept the things that come from the Spirit of God, for they are foolishness to him, and he cannot understand them, because they are spiritually discerned. The spiritual man makes judgments about all things, but he himself is not subject to any man's judgment.
> For who has known the mind of the Lord that he may instruct him? But we have the mind of Christ.
>
> —1 Corinthians 2:6-16

I've known illiterate and uneducated people who had uncommon wisdom and common sense about them. I've known people who seem willfully ignorant who are neither interested in knowledge, understanding, or wisdom. I've known intelligent people who seemingly have no wisdom or commonsense about them. And, of course, I've known literate people who have uncommon common sense and wisdom.

Remember the question earlier in the book about if we had the wisdom to ask what would our request be? And the freedom of choice was the answer? Well this godly wisdom we speak of is not about understanding physics, or Mathematics, or trivia, it is exercising our freedom of choice by accepting God's grand call of salvation and with it, join Him in the unspeakable mysteries of God's kingdom.

Prayer

Prayer has a significant place in the power of choice. It is a grace and a privilege and gift from God, which allows us to have direct access to the throne of the Almighty. Can you imagine that…the opportunity to talk to God Himself, and have Him hear us and answer us and care about us? "Call on me I will answer thee and show thee great and mighty things which thou knowest not" as Jeremiah says about God. Prayer changes things. That's what the Bible teaches us. We can have influence in the things of the world. We can ask God to move on behalf of other people and in our own lives.

True prayer is spiritually and physically healthful. It takes the emphasis off self and our needs and puts it on God and on to other people. It puts God as the primary object of our thinking and puts people as second in line. God's perfect will for us is that we will not be conformed to the ways of the world, but offer our selves as agents of good, which is holy and pleasing to God. We do this by the transformation of our mind from an earthly focus to the heavenly. It doesn't mean that we should be so heavenly that we are no earthly good, but it means we live a God-focused life.

Prayer logically follows the categories of seeking, knocking, and asking. It is one of the elements of our petitions to God. God knows what we need before we even ask, but the power is in the asking. It transfers mere thought into action. Asking is more humbling than demanding.

Knocking is more respectful than banging. Seeking is more transforming than expecting.

We merely have to choose to do that. That's the power and the significance and responsibility of choosing. I will choose to pray. I will choose to read the Bible. I will choose to do unto others as I would have them do to me. I will love those around me. I will love God with all my heart, mind, and soul.

Now that is choosing.

CHAPTER 16

THE DOING

A man who wants to do something will find a way; a man who doesn't will find an excuse.

—Stephen Dolley, Jr.

THIS BOOK INTENDS to describe the significance of the power of choice and the resulting effects (good and bad), it has on individuals and society. Down through history the power of choosing for one individual created world-altering events. Some of these are described in the context of this book, but others, like George Washington Carver, Leonardo Da Vinci, Christopher Columbus, Albert Schweitzer, the founders of our country (Washington, Jefferson, Adams, Franklin), Jonas Salk, to name just a few, all had dreams and visions of a better world and set about to create good.

Obviously and conversely, evil men have similar dreams, but the outcome is to the detriment of society: like the Stalins, the Hitlers, the Lenins, the Husseins, the philosophical ideals of a demeaning society (communism, slavery, oppression). Those had dire consequences.

Now leaves the doing. Armed with explanations, the tools, the significance of choice, and the willingness to step forth into the world with our renewed and fresh insight, there comes the phrase, "Just Do It." That should be our philosophy as it relates generally to life and specifically to choice. Just do! Find every opportunity to do, to look, experience, explore, discover, read, and acquire knowledge. You can learn from anyone. I have had about fifteen separate jobs in my 50-plus years of work life and each one has equipped me with the experience and tools to do other things. Each one, no matter how menial, brought invaluable experience into every other job and to every aspect of life. Oh, I've said the words many times to myself and others of what good is algebra, or this and that job, or even the dreaded words, I'm bored, but looking back now, each has broadened my knowledge and experience. And as for being bored, I don't see how that is possible.

So just do. Just pray, seek, knock, ask, use common sense, apply wisdom, do right, foster good habits, equip yourself with the tools of good thinking, and all these will enable you to make good choices. Recognize the fact that choices you make affect yourself and others. And, thank God for the blessing of free choice. The alternative is not pleasant. This diversity of appreciation of life and what life has to offer can only come about with an open mind.

Stewardship

When we recognize that we are caretakers of what has been given to us and that we are only passing through this world for a short time, we are more apt to be responsible workers, companions, friends, spouses, stewards of the environment, and good neighbors. There can be no other defining purpose in our lives than being committed to stewardship— service to God, our family, the community, and ourselves. It is our Christian duty to be a good steward. Often the religious community is lax in that regard. We put our efforts in spreading our faith, but neglect other elements of stewardship.

As aforementioned, we, the occupiers of the planet, have an awesome responsibility to sustain, protect, nurture, and treasure our only home. There is a heightened awareness of the urgency of addressing the issues of fossil fuel consumption, pollution, clean water, and keeping the food chain pure. Global warming, an often debated topic, is thought to be a crucial survival issue for the inhabitants of the earth. If not taken seriously, rising sea levels can consume beaches, towns, and initiate severe climatic change.

There is a growing consciousness to look toward alternative fuels, alternative energy, and a sustainable environment. There is much work being done and much more to do. When some countries having 20% of the population consuming 40% of the world's fuel reserves, then much needs to be done. Education and awareness are key to having every individual be a good steward of the earth. The planet depends upon it.

Be a good steward: Go Green—recycle (there are a host of recycling programs), conserve fresh water, consolidate trips, walk, buy energy saving products, and the list goes on.

Stewardship is more than protecting the environment—it is an important part, of course—but mostly it is about service. Service to others: the poor and unfortunate, the community, the church, and to our God. Where much is given, much is required of us. We are blessed with abundance in this country and we can use that gift of abundance to be of service to others.

Stewardship and choice? Yes, to be a good steward is a conscious choice. It is part of the doing. The doing is service and service is what is required of us. To repeat the scriptural verse of Micah, the Lord has required us to act justly (do what is right), show mercy (treat others as you wish to be treated), and lastly, to walk humbly with God. That is the doing. That is service. That is stewardship.

Peace

Blessed are the peacemakers for they shall be called the children of God.
—Matthew 5: 9

On the surface, peace sounds like a passive word, but being a peacemaker is very much being the activist. Two individuals come to mind as being the epitome of activism through peaceful efforts: Martin Luther King, Jr., and Mahatma Gandhi. There are others of course, many others (95 individuals and 20 organizations since 1901 who won the Nobel Peace Prize), who raised the voice of passive resistance to the tyrannies and oppressions of mankind. These two individuals, however, led radical change through peaceful means. Martin Luther King led the mass struggle for racial equality, and Mahatma Gandhi by gaining independence for India from British oppression. That doesn't mean those peace movements were without hardships and bloodshed, but the philosophies of such movements were of peaceful intent.

From the outset of our lives we can choose to be a peacemaker or not. In some circumstances it may be more difficult than others. For instance, it's easier to be one on a farm in Kansas versus the streets of a big city. Nevertheless we can have an attitude of peace. We can be at peace with ourselves, our fellow men, and God.

Isn't peace capsulated in the phrase, Do unto others as we would have them do to us?

In the choosing and in the worldview, what can the individual do? Even if we are at peace with ourselves, that alone is one individual with enormous power. We are a contributor to the betterment of the world and not evil.

Can't we each say that real peace begins within? Remember the power of multiplication? And, what power that has when the collective "us" have that attitude of being a peacemaker?

This is a deliberate choice. Will we say, from this moment on, in every circumstance of my life, I will be a person of peace? I will be at peace with my spouse, my parents, my children, my superiors, my neighbor, and my God.

> Lord, make me an instrument of your peace;
> Where there is hatred let me sow love,
> Where there is injury, pardon;
> Where there is doubt, faith;
> Where there is despair, hope;
> Where there is darkness, light;
> Where there is sadness, joy.
> Divine Master,
> Grant that I may not so much seek to be consoled as to console,
> To be understood as to understand,
> To be loved as to love,
> For it is in giving that we receive,
> It is in pardoning that we are pardoned
> And it is in dying that we are born to eternal life.

> St. Francis of Assisi

CHAPTER 17

CONCLUSION

THE GODLY TRANSFORMATION of our minds, our hearts, and our attitudes will refine our choices for the betterment of mankind, our own individual lives and thus the world.

Through our choices, it is altogether fitting that we should submit and dedicate ourselves to the will of God. Only by that submissive will, will our choices be directed and performed for His purposes. The apostle Paul says in his letter to the Romans:

> *Therefore, I urge you, brothers, in view of God's mercy, to offer your bodies as living sacrifices, holy and pleasing to God—this is your spiritual act of worship (your reasonable service, the expected responsibility). Do not conform any longer to the pattern of this world, but be transformed by the renewing of your mind. Then you will be able to test and approve what God's will is—his good, pleasing and perfect will.*
> —Romans 12:1-2

The act of transforming ourselves is the process; the renewing of our minds is our deliberate choice. Without which, there can be no metamorphosis of our spirit from the worldly to the spiritual.

We have by now established the fact that our choices, our decisions, and our purposes have profound impact on us as individuals and thus on our friends, family, community, church, and the whole of mankind.

However small we think our choices are will be multiplied a hundredfold in the larger scheme of things. "Our actions run as causes and return to us as results." We may be a link in a chain, a ball in a bearing, a voice crying in the wilderness, but if that link is missing, that ball ungreased, and the cry unfulfilled, then the human race suffers.

Once a work associate illustrated the point of how unimportant we are in the scheme of things (the company, society, the world), by saying, "What happens when you take your hand out of the bucket of water? Nothing! It is like it was never there." It was his way of saying if we were not here (not in the company, society, the world), it wouldn't make a bit of difference. *Au contraire* my friends, the level of the water in the bucket is greatly diminished. The contribution to society, to life, to family, and friends is greatly diminished.

John Donne in his poem, "No Man Is an Island" is more poignant:

No man is and island, entire of itself; every man is a piece of the continent, a part of the main. If a clod be washed away by the sea, Europe is the less, as well as if a promontory were, as well as if a manor of thy friend's or of thine own were: any man's death diminishes me, because I am involve in mankind, and therefore never send to know of whom the bell tolls; it tolls for thee.

Our choices have consequences both for us and others. The "others" may be in the broadest sense of the word, our family, friends, community, workplace, or world; or, for us. Rarely can we make decisions that only affect just us. Is there any decision we make that does not affect others directly or indirectly?

If we recognize that we have an effect on the world, however small or large that may be, then in some minute way, we influence others by doing good, corrupting, polluting, helping, encouraging, being a peacemaker, doing harm, hating, loving, solving problems… then we are on the road to knowing that "our lives are connected by a thousand invisible threads." It is a matter of choice—for good and for evil.

CONCLUSION

The conclusion of the matter of choice is, and there is no more fitting conclusion, the words of Solomon in Ecclesiastes 12:13 where he says:

> Now all has been heard; here is the conclusion of the matter: Fear God and keep his commandments, for this is the whole duty of man.

RESOURCE MATERIAL

Man's Search for Meaning, Vicktor Frankl.

Nineteen Eighty Four, George Orwell.

The Providence of God, video series, R. C. Sproul.

Attitude Is your Paintbrush, James W. Moore.

The Closing of the American Mind, Allan Bloom.

The Epic of America, James Trislow Adams.

George Washington Carver, The Man Who Overcame, Lawrence Elliott, 1966.

Collapse, Jared Diamond.

Come On People, Bill Cosby and Alvin F. Poussaint, M.D., 2007, Thomas Nelson, Inc.

BIBLIOGRAPHY

Adams, James Truslow. *The Epic of America;* Garden City, NY: Garden City Books 1931.

Albright, Madeleine. *The Mighty and the Almighty;* HarperCollins Publishers, New York, 2006.

Avraham, Regina. *Substance Abuse Prevention and Treatment*; Chelsea House Publishers, New York, 1988.

Warren, Rick. *The Purpose Driven Life;* Grand Rapids, MI : Zondervan, 2002.

Bellah, Robert N. *Habits of the Heart,* New York, NY, Harper & Row, 1985.

Bloom, Allan. *The Closing of the American Mind;* New York, NY; Simon and Schuster, 1987.

Carnegie, Dale. *How To Win Friends & Influence People;* Pocket Books, rev. ed., 1981, New York.

Clark, Ronald W. *Edison;* New York, Putnum's Sons, 1977.

Douglas, Frederick. *My Bondage and My Freedom;* Barnes & Noble, NY, 2005.

Fletcher, Joseph. *Situation Ethics;* The Westminster Press, Philadelphia, 1966.

Kushner, Harold S. *When Bad Things Happen to Good People;* Schocken Books, NY, 1981.

Lawson, Robert & Carol. *Chances Are...;* West Chester, PA: Chrysalis Books, 2002.

Levitt, Steven D. and Dubner, Stephen J. *Freakonomics;* Harper Collins Publishers, New York 2005.

Manguel, Alberto. *A History of Reading;* Viking Penguin, New York, 1996.

Meacham, Jon. *American Gospel;* Random House, New York, 2006.

Merzaros, Murry. *The Best of Luck;* Akron, OH, AM Media, 1996.

Mlodinow, Leonard. *The Drunkard's Walk;* Pantheon Books, New York, 2008.

Schaler, Jeffery A., PH.D. *Addiction is a Choice;* Open Court, Chicago, 2000.

Sides, Hampton. *Ghost Soldiers;* Doubleday, New York, 2001.

Simonds, John Ormbee. *Landscape Architecture;* 2nd ed.; McGraw-Hill, Inc., New York, 1983.

Tuchman, Barbara W. *The March of Folly;* Alfred A. Knopf, NewYork, 1984.

White, Michael. *Soul Catcher;* HarperCollins, New York, 2007.

PW

LaVergne, TN USA
10 May 2010
182204LV00007B/239/P